GW00505036

The Dreamer ́s Guide to
Running a Country
Restaurant

ELSIE AND ALAN PICHEL-JUAN

To Helm
With all good wishes
Elsie Pichel-Juan

The Dreams, The Realities

Dreamer's Guides™
Breese Books, London

Published by Dreamer's Guides™
Breese Books Limited
164 Kensington Park Road
London W11 2ER

ISBN: 0 947533 61 3

Typeset in 10 / 12pt Palatino and Ottawa by
Ann Buchan (Typesetters) Middlesex
Printed in Great Britain by
Itchen Printers Limited, Southampton

CONTENTS

CHAPTER ONE

THE DREAM

The warm night air stirs the rose-patterned curtains at the open casement windows, shimmering the moonlight reflected on the uneven leaded panes. All is quiet except for the faint hooting of an owl in the distance, the creak of the ancient timbers gently easing muscles cramped by centuries of stress and the somewhat less romantic gurgle of pipes in the bathroom along the corridor. It is three a.m.

'You awake?' The man's voice asks softly.
  'Mmm.' The woman's voice is drowsy but receptive.
  'Lovely old place, isn't it?'
  'Gorgeous.'
  'The meal was good too.'
  'Wouldn't it be marvellous to live in a place like this?'
  'All those fabulous beams and crooked old floors.'
  'We must come back in winter and sit by a roaring fire in that inglenook fireplace.'
  'I could enjoy running a place like this. How about you?'
  'I can just imagine it. All our friends could come for weekends.'
  'And birthdays and anniversaries.'
  'Entertaining on a grand scale. A bit like a country house-party.'
  'It would be hard work, though.'
  'Only at first. Once we'd got it running we'd hire staff to do the work. Then we'd be free to welcome the customers and be sociable.'
  'I wonder what a place like this would cost?'
  'A lot more than we could raise.'
  'Maybe we could rent something to begin with; until we'd made enough to buy a place of our own.'
  'How much will you get when you leave the Service next year?'

'Not sure exactly. It should be a fair bit.'

'We'll still need to earn some money when you retire and I must confess this appeals to me.'

'Me too.'

At nine o'clock the next morning 'the dream' has taken a firm hold. The owner of the inn, who had tumbled gratefully into bed shortly before four a.m. and left it again before seven, because the part-time staff had granted themselves a well-deserved (their opinion) Sunday morning lie in, has made the grave error of stopping beside the dreamers' table to inquire if everything is satisfactory.

Dirty dishes are piling up in the kitchen; his wife is juggling pots and pans, making more toast and coffee, preparing vegetables for lunch and hoping desperately that the chef will turn up on time. The elderly housemaid — their only live-in 'treasure' — is hovering impotently, unable to clean the bedrooms or vacuum the dining-room floor until breakfast is out of the way. Our dreamers are in full flight of fancy — gushing overblown compliments and pumping the harassed landlord for every snippet of information they can extract.

Wearily he recognizes the symptoms: about-to-retire officer and wife, soon to find themselves in the state of relative affluence that accompanies the severance lump-sum; pondering the direction of their future and lured by the siren-song of the country idyll that the old inn represents so poignantly.

The landlord has seen it all before; he has probably even been there himself. He does not wish them ill, just that they would take their fantasy elsewhere and let him get on with preparing for the invasion of the Sunday lunchtime hordes.

'The landlord looked tired, I thought.'

'He did. Probably stayed up drinking until all hours.'

'Not got his staff properly organized yet. That was his wife in the kitchen cooking breakfast, from what he said.'

'It will be a really great place once it's running properly. We must come again.'

'I think I'll contact a few estate agents tomorrow — just to get an idea of the sort of money involved.'

The dream has many different manifestations; this particular version of it is the most extreme and dangerously potent. Perhaps there is something in the fabric of old buildings that casts its spell just at that moment when the potential innkeeper/restaurateur, well-dined and generously-wined, is at his most vulnerable to suggestion.

We, too, fell beneath that same spell and it took us thirty years to break free of it. The love affair with the medieval hostelry is all too common, but if it is to develop into a lasting relationship the love must be genuine, deep and selfless; mere infatuation is not enough.

Ancient houses are hard work, demand unlimited time and energy and resemble nothing so much as bottomless pits into which money is sucked down without you even having the dubious satisfaction of throwing it.

The initial cost of buying them is generally high, precisely because of their universal appeal. Should a bargain present itself, think very carefully before you seize it with both hands; it is more than possible that the cost of keeping it from falling down will wipe out whatever is left of your resources.

The cost of insuring them, too, is higher than for a modern building of comparable size: (a) because, with all that timber and the impossibility of burying the electric wiring out of harm's way, they are a fire hazard; (b) because the original — or at any rate antique — doors and windows are a security man's nightmare, and even if you can bring yourself to permit their disfigurement by modern locks, bolts, latches, chains and burglar alarms, there are still the leaded panes as a standing invitation for the rankest amateur burglar armed with a pocket-knife; (c) because the uneven floors, head-bangingly-low doors and creaking, twisting staircases contribute substantially to the incidence of accident claims from careless customers.

And if you have fallen for the ultimate folly of a thatched roof then a second — perhaps even a third — mortgage may be necessary to meet the premiums.

Assuming that, undaunted by all this doom-mongering, you find your dream house and go ahead and buy it, there are plenty more obstacles to negotiate. Not insignificant among these is the labyrinth of legislation enacted for the protection of historic buildings.

In the course of conveyancing the property your solicitor will acquaint you with its precise status:

'It's Grade II listed, you realize?'

'Really? How exciting! We are about to buy a chunk of history — a piece of our National Heritage.'

As most solicitors do pretty well out of conveyancing he is unlikely to risk disillusioning you by pointing out the disadvantages involved. You will find out all about them the hard way when the inspector from the Department of Health and Safety insists that you make improvements to your premises to bring them in line with the hygiene and safety regulations, and the Planning Department refuses your application on the grounds that the proposed alterations conflict with the laws designed to protect 'listed' buildings from unsuitable changes.

Your piece of history will fall into one of two categories: either it is still in its primitive state or has already been 'restored', with suitably discreet mock oil-lamps on the walls, small-bore central-heating (burning fuel and money in roughly equal proportions in the never-ending battle with draughts from unexpected sources, like the gaps between your picturesque, creaky floor-boards) and bathrooms with appealing, contorted beams that act as magnets for dust and cobwebs and soap-splashes, and tufts of hair from the heads of unwary, tall guests.

Let us deal first with the already restored version. Once the first, fine, careless rapture has given way to something more nearly approaching realism, you will quickly arrive at the conclusion that the modernization was, at best, the work of a gross incompetent. Certain aspects may even convince you that feeble-minded malevolence also played a part.

It is too late. You will just have to keep your imagination on a tight rein.

If you are sensible (unlikely, since you have already committed the folly of buying the place) you will learn to live with it the way it is. However obvious it may be, to anyone with a grain of common-sense, that only a congenital idiot would have sited the bath so that the door crashes against it every time someone enters, the cost of moving it will almost certainly be prohibitive and the attempt may well prove futile into the bargain.

A little phrase we learned to heed, in the wake of several disastrously ill-considered undertakings, was: 'You never know what you will find in these old houses.'

It is uttered by plumbers, heating engineers, carpenters and others as an excuse for not giving you a proper estimate for the job you have called them in to do.

They are not referring to hoards of gold coins, nor yet to priest-holes and secret passages; the surprises they have in mind come in the shape of massive beams which block the passage of waste-pipes, and original medieval walls made out of thin, bark-covered lengths of green wood, criss-crossed with springy laths, coated with a primitive combination of horsehair and cow-dung and covered, to an impressive depth, by several centuries-worth of yearly whitewashing. This stuff weighs almost as much as an equivalent amount of lead and, if injudiciously disturbed, tends to crash to the floor and disintegrate in an all-pervading cloud of dark grey dust that stings the eyes and clogs the throat, and the floor-boards, for days after.

There are many other examples we could cite but these will give you the general picture. The incompetent builder, all too often, turns out to have had his reasons.

We turn next to the primitive version — the one the estate agent describes as 'eminently suitable for restoration'.

This alternative allows you to make your own blunders but, when a guest remarks that the bath should have been sited on the opposite wall, robs you of the chance to blame the error on the idiot who did the installation long before you bought the place.

The cost of this option is unlikely to be less than that of buying the *fait accompli* and what is more, there is no known way of finding out in advance precisely what you are letting yourself in for. Any estimate you manage to wring from your builder will be couched in such vague and elastic terms that it does not bind him in any way, either with regard to money or to time. Your only absolute certainty is that the ultimate amount you are obliged to part with will never be less than his quote. If you try to insist that he commit himself to something a little more concrete, he will shake his head and say, 'You never know what you will find, etc.'

If you decide to put your faith in an architect, be sure to choose one who has a life-time's experience of timber-framed constructions; he, too, will be uncertain of what he is going to find, but will make a better stab at guessing than the man whose practical knowledge is confined to modern structures.

The same applies even more strongly to your builder. Builders with long experience of the *genre* develop an instinct for what is best left alone but, before allowing them to begin the work, even these should be frisked for spirit-levels, set-squares and plumb-lines — instruments which are strictly taboo in a timber-frame setting.

Early in our own venture we needed a doorway knocked through a wall to connect two rooms, and chose for the job a carpenter who came highly recommended for his skill, speed and punctuality. He arrived on the dot of eight-thirty and finished in record time. The work was impeccably done, the finish smooth and beyond reproach, but the doorway leaned at the strangest angle, several inches out of true.

'You've put it in crooked,' we accused, and he shook his head, mortally offended.

'I measured it most carefully — it's absolutely straight.' He took out his spirit level and proved to our dissatisfaction that what he said was correct. The doorway was as vertically true as it was horizontally accurate. It was the house that leaned at an angle.

That doorway irritated us for years until we finally salvaged some crooked timbers from a demolished barn and superimposed them upon its carefully-squared frame.

Doing-It-Yourself is definitely best avoided unless you have lived in a timber house for a very long time and have had the opportunity to watch the experts at work. Not only does the unpractised amateur not know what he might find, he is also unlikely to recognize it when he has found it.

Two kinds of people try this option: the first quickly become discouraged and either call in professional help or pack in the idea altogether: the second become so involved in the project, so fascinated by the old craft techniques and so spellbound by the magic of the historic wood that they turn into perfectionists and lavish so much time and love on the restoration work that they never actually get around to opening the restaurant.

Well, that gets Ye Olde Coaching Inne out of the way, though we would offer a word of warning to those who have refused to be put off by our doom-mongering: the beauty of the surroundings will attract the customers initially; how soon — and how often — they return depends on the talents and personality of 'Mine Host' and his partner.

CHAPTER TWO

MAKING THE DECISION

So you want to run a restaurant?

Why?

If the honest answer to that question is because you have a glamorized picture of the social life, and a high expectation of the financial rewards, your dream needs to be subjected to some pretty hard-hitting analysis.

The harsh truth is that those evenings when you bask in the compliments lavished upon your efforts by charming and delightful customers, flattered to have you sit for a short period at their table and entertain them with your brilliant conversation, will be grossly outnumbered by times when the chef is in a bad mood, the diners are difficult and you are exhausted because the part-time waiters didn't turn up and you have had to do their work as well as your own.

As to the financial rewards, these are never a foregone conclusion. There are several fairly accurate methods of estimating what your turnover is likely to be, but patronizing a popular establishment and multiplying your bill by the number of fellow diners is not one of them. It might give you a rough idea of how much money has changed hands, but will tell you nothing about what proportion of that goes into the proprietor's pocket, and how much he is obliged to squander on purchasing stock and paying overheads and wages — to say nothing of servicing a mortgage large enough to make the eyes water.

Assuming that your motives are rather more commendable than this — and more down-to-earth — then the next question is: what kind of a restaurant do you wish to run?

Examine your dream very carefully before committing yourself on this one; if subdued lighting, and candles casting a romantic glow on immaculate linen, sparkling glass and good silver, feature prominently in it then you are only going to be happy running the corner caff if there is a very real prospect of quickly upgrading it. (This may seem ridiculously self-evident but as the hunt for suitable premises drags on, and the perfect house of your dreams recedes into the realms of the unattainable, your perspective may become warped and logic and common-sense desert you.)

If you have not already done so, this is a good time to engage in some serious comparisons with your partner to make absolutely certain that your individual dreams, if not identical, are at least compatible. If the result of this exercise in dream-swapping is unpalatable, console yourself with the thought that it would have been far worse coming when you were already committed and up to your ears in debt and dirty dishes.

One of the first among those essentials that need to be defined is the absolute minimum in the way of premises that will satisfy you both. Even if you are prepared to consider a wide range of options there are nevertheless bound to be certain standards below which you will not go. Once you have established these you can then take stock of your assets and calculate whether they come anywhere near to the outlay needed.

Calculating the size of your bank-balance doesn't usually present any great problem; establishing the maximum extent to which it can be augmented with overdrafts and loans will need all the charm and powers of persuasion that you can muster.

If you own a house and propose to sell it to finance your venture, then you will need to know its precise value — and, more importantly, how much it can reasonably be expected to fetch within the time-scale of your plans. The two sums do not always coincide. For this purpose the opinion of two estate agents is better than one, and that of half-a-dozen better still.

You should also, at this stage, try to find a sympathetic ear to bend regarding the feasibility of obtaining a mortgage — though preferably not that of your bank-manager who, in these computerized days, probably has an inflated view of the monetary value of his time. Only when you have all this information in your grasp will you be in a position to see what kind of property is likely to be within your price-range.

Establishing these parameters before you start restaurant-hunting will save time, avoid futile journeys, and shield you from the heart-break of finding the picture-postcard answer to your wildest dreams and rushing off in a frenzy of excitement to tell all your friends about it, then being forced to admit, once you have gone over your calculations one more time, that it is right out of your league.

Looking at options which are beyond your means is terribly demoralizing. We know; we've been there and wept buckets. In the first flush of enthusiasm our hearts, and almost our spirits, were broken by an unbelievably attractive country house in five acres of mature grounds, which had everything, including a couple of staff cottages and a ballroom hung with opulent crystal chandeliers. The worst part of our disappointment was the fact that it was a tremendous bargain — for anyone with approximately twice the amount of capital that we were able to raise.

The cost of buying your premises is only the beginning. There will be a great many other demands on your rapidly diminishing resources: bills for the obscure, but legally required, services performed by your solicitor, stamp duty levied by the government at the rate of 1 per cent of the purchase price, fees for surveying, et cetera. There are also a host of other items of expenditure to take into account. You will need, for example, to have some idea of what your yearly outgoings will amount to: rates, insurance, fuel bills, water charges, licences — you can't rely on the income from your business being sufficient to take care of them right from the start. A reasonable balance of capital left over after the initial payments have been made is essential to your peace of mind and probably to your survival as a restaurateur.

A substantial item which must be included in your day-to-day expenses is your wages bill, and the highest earner on your staff will certainly be the chef. If, therefore, you or your partner can cope with the cooking (the ability to micro-wave commercially prepared frozen food doesn't count as a qualification) it will effect a welcome saving on your total wages budget. It is advisable anyway, for complete begin-ners, to start off with no more than the indispensable minimum of paid help; generally speaking, trained staff tend to be disdainful of amateur proprietors and rarely give of their best for them, while the untrained need tuition and super-vision and you won't be able to give this while you are still floundering around, trying to learn the job yourself.

Your final choice could well be influenced by the extent to which you can cut the outgoings down to size. The differ-ence between insisting on a well-staffed inn with Dickensian connections and being prepared to do most of the work yourself in more modern, less demanding surroundings — relying on your own charisma and talent to pull in the punters — could mean the difference between becoming a successful restaurateur and remaining a dreamer.

Only when all these facts and figures are firmly fixed in your mind will you be in a position to judge whether a proposition is viable and whether you have any hope of making it work well enough to pay off your debts before you are too old and too exhausted to reap the benefits.

A small word of warning — the fact that you have man-aged to sweet-talk some financial institution into stumping up the mega-mortgage you need to acquire your dream is not an iron-clad guarantee that you will make enough mon-ey to cover the repayments. It certifies only that the property itself represents sufficient value to indemnify the bank — or whatever — in the unhappy event of you being unable to meet your obligations.

Should all this delving into your financial status lead you to the inescapable conclusion that it is just not enough to buy your dream, however nimbly you juggle figures around, there is no need to accept the inevitability of a rude, disillu-sioned awakening just yet — there are a couple of other alternatives available to you.

Renting is the cheaper of these options, though it will

probably seriously limit your choice. You could be successful in obtaining the tenancy of a country pub, though this is
no longer the cheap sinecure it used to be when we started
up in the business, thirty-five years ago, and the modest
local authority rates demand for the property was more
than twice what we paid in rent to the brewery. Other than
that you will have to search very hard to find a business to
rent in the depth of the country, but small market towns are
an attractive near-equivalent, and often contain premises to
rent at quite reasonable rates.

Leasing, from the point of view of initial outlay, is the
middle option and there are still leases available — despite
legislation in this area in recent years — again usually to be
found in small market towns rather than truly rural villages.
Some breweries nowadays are offering mid-term leasing as
an alternative to the more usual tenancy agreements, which
run from year to year.

These arrangements still need quite a substantial cash
sum and involve fairly high yearly rentals, as well as limiting the freedom of lessees to choose their suppliers of alcoholic
drinks, but they are worth looking into if you are not able to
buy the kind of premises you have set your heart on.

Those leasing agreements that we have had the opportunity to examine offer the additional advantage of help in the
form of training and back-up services which not only ease
the learning process but also lessen the 'risk' factor inherent
in going it entirely alone.

The normal length of the lease you are required to buy is
about twenty years but they make provisions for it to be sold
on, or ceded, after an initial, qualifying period, thus allowing you to consolidate your own position and, if you are
successful financially in this venture, to move on to buying
that coveted place of your own.

CHAPTER THREE

LOCATION

The sun is sparkling on the water beneath the terrace of the riverside pub where the dreamers are eating a leisurely lunch. The attractive setting has set them off again.

'How do you feel about buying a place by the river?'

'Oh yes! I could be deliriously happy in a riverside pub! Marvellous idea.'

'We'd serve drinks under bright umbrellas on our own private stretch of the river bank.'

'And ducks! We must have ducks; they're so comical I could watch them all day.'

The riverside pub creates a charming image. Like the oak beams and thatched roof it is irresistibly seductive and the focus of a great many dreams. And perhaps on a dozen days in the year it may even come close to living up to the image the dreamer has of it. It is also very attractive from a trade point of view and, sensibly run, it can do very well indeed and, consequently, the cost of buying such property tends to be higher than for a comparable place without water-frontage.

If this is not the case, then there is undoubtedly a very good or, more probably, a very bad reason why. Vulnerability to flooding in the wet seasons is the obvious candidate. This drawback, serious though it is, need not automatically discount it as a proposition; personally we know of several successful riverside — and harbourside — hostelries that flood at regular intervals and continue to flourish, despite the expense and inconvenience of these incursions.

With a sufficiently brisk summer trade they can afford to close up the establishment and drag the furniture upstairs during the worst of the winter. Forewarned is forearmed with sandbags, wellington boots and carpets that can be whipped up at a moment's notice and stored out of harm's way, above the highest water mark.

Discreet questioning of the locals will fairly certainly unleash a (metaphorical) flood of horror stories, gleefully embellished, of natural disasters that have engulfed the region in the past. Such interrogations, however, are better carried out well before you show any interest in buying the property; some country folk have a quaint sense of what is amusing and, if aware of your intentions, are quite capable of swearing that the river has never been known to flood, just for the pleasure of laughing at you as you hang out your sodden carpets to dry.

If you find your haven by the water you would be wise to employ the best surveyor you can possibly afford; one who will delve deeply into the fabric of the building, bringing to light any structural deterioration caused by water in the past and giving you a realistic estimate of the damage that could result from possible future immersion.

Careful research should also be carried out into any local developments, actual or planned, which could have an effect on the river levels, such as alterations to bridges, locks and dams, or any of those curious fabrications dreamed up by the alchemists at the water board for the purpose of converting water (for you) into money (for them).

It would be difficult to listen to too many accounts of what is going on in the area, even if most of them are conflicting, and you will eventually learn to distinguish between the informed opinion, pious prejudice and blatant self-interest that constitute local politics.

You should also check at the local council offices to find out if there are any special by-laws governing riverside locations, such as rights of way and the protection of waterfowl. Rights of way can be a great nuisance in any location but are particularly disruptive if you own the land right to the water and wish to use it as a pleasant summer facility.

In the course of conducting the searches which form part of the conveyancing process, your solicitor should turn up any such restrictions to your right to enjoy your property 'without let or hindrance', as the quaint legal phraseology has it. Our own experience, however, has taught us the wisdom of being alert to the possibility of something being overlooked.

Another yawning pitfall is insurance. Insurers are notoriously reluctant to give sensible cover if a property is susceptible to flooding; and a bitterly cold February day, when you are knee-deep in water and facing the prospect of having to get along without further revenue until the rain has stopped and the place dried out, is the worst possible time to start sorting out the exclusion clauses in your policy.

Whether you choose the river, or coastal, or any other environment, the nature of the establishment you have in mind will play a part in deciding where to concentrate your search. The district you choose should, ideally, contain a large number of the type of people you are hoping to attract, even if you do expect the bulk of your custom to come out from London, or other population centres; the locals are the ones who will keep you going during the worst of the winter. A good local clientele is a year-round asset and much more easily — and cheaply — canvassed for those 'special evenings' that dire need prompts you to organize to boost your takings when trade is in the doldrums.

An area which already has a flourishing, popular restaurant in it is not the best place to start looking, unless the surrounding population is large enough, and affluent enough, to support both enterprises. Market forces — as the media now call old-fashioned competition — are marvellous news for the consumer, but less so for those who provide the goods or services, and once set up in business you will have crossed the great divide and joined the latter category.

There are few experiences more galling to the conscientious restaurateur than watching from the window of his half-empty dining-room as his customers file into the rival establishment across the street, where they will be served inferior food at inflated prices.

An important reason for choosing a particular location could be the ready availability of supplies. A pub situated in an active fishing village will be able to offer ultra-fresh, locally caught fish as a speciality, for instance. Similarly, produce delivered daily from a good local organic market-garden could feature prominently on your menu in this vegetable-conscious era. And generally speaking, the less distance your supplies have to travel the fresher and cheaper they are, thus achieving quality and cost-control in happy combination.

When you have thoroughly explored and researched your chosen area, you can then, with a clear conscience, start on the really exciting part and contact every possible purveyor of the kind of business, or property, you intend to buy. This includes informing the local estate agents of your requirements (together with a firm indication of your upper financial limit, which they will make a point of ignoring), buying all the local and national newspapers that carry advertisements of businesses for sale, and taking out subscriptions to some of the host of magazines and papers pertinent to the catering trade.

An arrangement with your local recycling organization could save you from suffocating beneath the mountain of paper that is destined to accumulate during this phase.

It is almost inevitable that the house of your dreams will be there amongst the first dozen or so properties that you inspect. The perfect solution has a knack of appearing on the market with the sort of coincidental timing that convinces you beyond all doubt that fate intended it just for you. Running concurrently with this joyous conviction will be an uneasy disbelief that it has all happened so quickly and effortlessly. Hold on firmly to that disbelief.

When the excitement has died down it will help you to accept what you should have realized all along — that, perfect though it appears, your restaurant (or old mill/redundant vicarage/disinherited manor house) is either too large, too small, too mouldering, too expensive (the most likely defect) or in quite the wrong place. The sad truth is that the perfect building, in the ideal location, at a price you can afford, simply doesn't exist — unless your supply of money is unlimited. In which case why, in God's name, do you want to go in for something so overwhelmingly exacting as running a restaurant?

Those of us who have been through this have all been

forced to compromise on one or other of these criteria but, with patience and perseverance (and a hard-won immunity to the pleading, tear-stained faces of frustrated estate agents) it need not preclude an ultimately satisfactory outcome.

It is asking for trouble to buy a country property that you have seen only a few times for brief periods, under blazing sunshine, surrounded by flowers and gracefully drooping willow branches. That adorable country lane, winding between hedges starred with wild pink roses, could easily be transformed into a noisesome, impassable mud-slide by carts and tractors, come muck-spreading time.

And bear in mind too that, when you have finished converting your disused water-mill, so delightfully hidden from view in a back-water of the county's best kept village, the proud inhabitants will fight tooth and claw to prevent you from despoiling their prize-winning environment by erecting the indispensable sign without which even the most enterprising of customers will be unable to find you.

Our own first venture was a picturesque sixteenth-century village inn, part of which stood literally in the graveyard, no more than a dozen yards from the church porch. Charming, we thought, imagining the more up-market segment of the congregation calling in for a sherry after the service and perhaps being tempted to stay to lunch. Before signing the final, binding contract we paid it a score or more visits, in winter, spring and early summer but, due to an unfortunate oversight, none of these was on a Sunday; the local gossips, who regaled us with all manner of hair-raising tales about the neighbourhood, unfortunately omitted to mention that the vicar and his team of bell-ringers were possessed by the consuming ambition to ring their way into the *Guinness Book of Records* with the longest-lasting continuous peal ever to be inflicted on a parish.

Neither had it occurred to us that the tuneful, and powerful, Westminster chimes of the church clock, situated on the side of the tower close to what was destined to be our bedroom window, were going to wake us at fifteen-minute intervals throughout every night until the merciful day when the mechanism failed and the parish council was too mean, or too impoverished, to have it repaired.

I doubt if either of these things would have prevented us from taking the place but it would have been nice to know what we were getting into.

One can never hope to foresee all the possible snags but, by inspecting the property under the most widely varied conditions possible, you can limit the eventual shocks to the genuinely unpredictable.

Our family's earliest exponent of 'the dream' left his native shores at the end of the First World War for a career in the Colonial Service (a perfectly respectable thing to do in those days). He retired with a modest pension a few months before the outbreak of the Second World War and bought the country inn he had kept his sanity by dreaming about during his twenty-year absence: a small, comfortable hostelry in a hamlet of exactly one hundred souls. The handful of local customers made minimal demands on his time during the hours of required opening and the river meandered slowly by, a fisherman's short stroll from the front door.

When war was declared he found himself in the enviable position of being far from any area that was vulnerable to air attack, with enough land to grow ample vegetables, an orchard to provide fruit and adjacent outhouses suitable for keeping a pig and some chickens. He had hardly finished congratulating himself on his astute choice of location when the Ministry of Defence began the construction of three airfields within a four-mile radius of it. Right away his bar became the focus for the leisure hours of the construction workers and, when their job was finished and they had departed, the RAF filled the void with half-a-dozen bomber squadrons whose personnel flocked to the inn in their hundreds, in search of more congenial surroundings than the Nissen huts that housed them.

The gentle, lazy dream was transformed into a nightmare of long hours and never-ending toil — even counting the takings was a chore that kept him up far into the night. Short of a hot-line to the planners in the War Department, he could not possibly have foreseen this unwelcome yet profitable outcome.

CHAPTER FOUR

FINANCE

The options for financing your venture depend entirely on the type of premises you propose to buy, your business prospects and, to a degree, your own personal powers of persuasion.

The building society is unlikely to be much help; their mortgages are based on the value of the buildings involved and the assured income of the mortgagees — an all-important indicator of their ability to keep up the repayments or, in the case of endowment mortgages, the life-insurance premiums. The potential revenue from your business will be too much of an unknown quantity, in the early stages at any rate, to constitute a satisfactory guarantee.

Nowadays, too, a bank mortgage will also depend on the sound, physical value of those assets that can be foreclosed upon if the worst happens. Should you also need to borrow money to finance the expense of fitting-out your premises and all the other start-up costs, like removals, insurance, buying stock, et cetera, your bank-manager will take some convincing.

If you are buying a going concern, as against converting some other form of premises, you will almost certainly have to cough up a substantial sum in addition to the cost of the buildings, furnishings, equipment and stock, to cover the goodwill.

Goodwill is an intangible asset and is impossible to quantify accurately. To the vendor it represents the sum of all the hard work he has put in to attract customers in the first place and keep them happy and coming back regularly: the patience with which he has listened to their tedious anecdotes, tolerated their foibles, stood waiting on aching feet for them to finish their coffee, pay the bill and go home: the forbearance he has shown in the face of their trivial complaints, snide remarks and even downright rudeness. In his view he has tamed them, trained them, licked them into shape and, in consequence, he deserves a substantial monetary reward from the next incumbent — you — in recognition of all the benefits you will reap from his labours.

To you it represents, at best, a core of potential customers, a proportion of whom will resent the defection of your predecessor and never patronize the establishment again; the rest may come once to look you over and if they don't like you, or fail to appreciate what you have to offer, no amount of money paid out in the name of goodwill can bring them back.

It goes without saying that this transitory asset is lost without trace in the event of the business going under and, in consequence, is unlikely to be regarded as something upon which a sensible lender would be willing to advance hard cash.

Even in those instances where it represents a fair assessment of the standing the vendor enjoys with his clientele, it is an ethereal thing and can quickly evaporate under a new regime.

After a brief transition period the new owner creates his own following: this is particularly so in the kind of small business where the proprietor has his own individual style and maintains a high profile.

During the boom period, when the price of property rose steadily year by year, a great many banks and financial institutions were happy to offer large mortgages to small businesses — the difference between the loan and the tangible assets it purchased being rapidly bridged by the constant improvement in property values which it was almost universally assumed had become a guaranteed fact of modern financial life.

A large proportion of these lenders, however, withdrew from the market in the recession which followed. One set of figures we were shown suggested a drop of more than two-thirds since 1989. Those who remain willing to lend are only prepared to do so on the soundly-established value of the freehold involved. Even caterers with years of experience in the trade are finding it difficult to obtain loans for more than 60 per cent of the purchase price of a new hotel, restaurant or pub venture.

There are, however, finance houses that specialize in procuring backing for the purchase of restaurants, hotels, shops and other 'service' enterprises by arranging mortgages and other facilities. Where they are convinced that a proposition is sound and the projected returns satisfactory, they can obtain mortgages of up to 70 per cent of the purchase price of a going concern or 100 per cent of the freehold value.

Should you approach one of these for help, they will seek to establish the validity of your application by arranging to have the premises independently valued and preparing the exhaustive viability reports on the current and potential trading position of the business which are needed to convince their lenders that they are offering a safe investment. They will make a charge for these services, regardless of whether or not your application is eventually successful.

The same system applies also to leasehold properties, where the maximum loan can be up to 65 per cent of the cost. We mention, without comment, that all of the institutions who were good enough to supply us with information were (like certain politicians) cautiously optimistic about the possibility of an impending improvement in the economic climate.

* * *

If you have opted for the tenancy of a pub you will have to produce a lump sum to pay for the 'ingoing' — that is the value of the fixtures, fittings, furnishings and equipment. The amount will, of course, depend on the nature and quantity of all these things and, while you will be offered a reasonably close estimate of what it will come to by the landlords, the final figure will be decided by a valuation performed at the moment of exchange.

Your landlord will almost certainly insist on this sum being paid from your savings and not with borrowed money. It will be returned to you, courtesy of the new occupant and subject to a fresh valuation, when you relinquish the tenancy. The theoretical purpose of the procedure is to reward you for the care you have taken of the stuff and for any improvements you have made during your occupancy. It also keeps the local valuers in lucrative work.

An inventory will also be carried out of the stock to be found on the premises at the time of take-over, and the result charged to you at cost price (plus the ubiquitous VAT).

No matter how carefully you and your professional advisers have gone over all these figures there will always be surprises — or, more accurately, shocks — in store, so a small financial reserve is undoubtedly the dreamer's best insurance against finding his dreams replaced by endless sleepless nights.

CHAPTER FIVE

CUISINE — CHEF

Our dreamers have probably convinced themselves that the difference between cooking for thirty people and preparing a dinner-party for six, is merely a question of more food in bigger saucepans and employing a trainee chef to take care of the boring things like portion control and costing and how much to add in for seasoning. If so reality is waiting for them just around the corner, rolling-pin raised, ready to strike. She may be an exceptional cook, but recipes are only one of the things she needs to know about, and leaving vital matters like profit margin to an inexperienced employee is a guaranteed short cut to failure.

First of all, in a commercial setting your thirty people will rarely all sit down to eat at the same time; they are much more likely to arrive in twos and fours, order all manner of different dishes to be served simultaneously then, just when you've got everything ready to serve, decide to have another couple of gin and tonics with the party of friends who have just walked into the bar. The food that is either drying out or quietly congealing is your problem, not theirs.

The only advantage the dreamer-turned-professional will find is that of not having to whip off her apron and join the guests in the dining-room, trying to look as if she had never boiled so much as an egg in her entire life. The transition from dilettante to professional is possible — we and thousands of others have made it — but don't expect it to be easy, or disaster-free.

Organization is the key, both to success, and to keeping your sanity. Plan your menus in a way that eliminates all unnecessary strain on the kitchen. By all means offer your diners a properly balanced choice of dishes but, in addition to costing each one meticulously, you must work out the time and difficulty involved in its preparation, particularly in the final stages just prior to serving, and use this information when compiling your menus to ensure that they are not overloaded with labour-intensive items. This precaution will go a long way towards avoiding the log-jams that cause accidents and lost tempers in the kitchen and poor results and testy customers in the dining-room.

'Stick to what you can do really well' is the golden rule for that important dinner-party to which you invite the boss when promotions are in the air, and it is even more applicable in the commercial kitchen. Simple dishes, exquisitely executed, are far more impressive than ambitious near-misses.

The microwave oven is an invaluable tool — though reheated, pre-packed, commercially prepared dishes will definitely not pass muster in a quality restaurant.

On the other hand, vegetables that have been blanched and portioned before the rush began, can quickly be made ready for the table without supervision and with no loss of colour or texture. It is ideal, also, for rapidly bringing up to serving-temperature dishes like *Carbonades Flamande, Boeuf Bourguinon* and venison *civet* — the sort of dishes which are cooked slowly for a long time and are actually improved by re-heating. It is far from being the universal cooking tool that the manufacturers' promotional literature would have us believe but, sensibly used, it is a good, time-saving device.

Some years ago we called in for lunch at a country pub which served excellent simple food and were surprised to find their usual modest menu suddenly augmented by such high-flown additions as venison in a cream and calvados sauce, breast of guineafowl in white wine with green pepper, and casseroled grouse.

'They've got a French chef,' the whisper went around the community.

When a couple of other modest establishments in the area went similarly up-market we were struck by the remarkable coincidence that not only were they all offering the same dishes but these were printed in precisely the same order on their menus. Shortly after that the sales representative for a manufacturer of frozen foods left us a list of the latest line of dishes, specially prepared for the commercial kitchen, upon which we found the venison, guineafowl breasts, grouse, and all the other suddenly popular items. It also promised a supply of ready-printed menus — thoughtfully interspersed with spaces for the inclusion of the restaurant's own humble offerings — with the initial order.

The moral of this cautionary tale is: if you must use subterfuges such as these, at least show a little originality in disguising their origins. Subterfuge, on principle, should be avoided wherever possible, first of all to avoid conflict with the Trade Descriptions Act, but also because if your customers catch you out they will never trust you again.

A prime example to illustrate this point is to be found in our experience at a restaurant which had just finished stocking its newly-acquired vivarium with prime, costly lobsters brought down from Scotland at enormous expense. We accepted the pressing invitation of the head waiter, chose the beast which most took our fancy and despatched it to the chef with recommendations for the way we wanted it cooked. In a remarkably short space of time, a splendid salver, bearing Lobster *Thermidor* on the half shell was ceremoniously carried in and placed before us.

The dish was acceptable but frankly disappointing — somehow that unmistakable, straight-out-of-the-sea freshness had got lost in the short distance between kitchen and table. The waiter who cleared our plates was pretty second-rate too — he clumsily let one of the empty shells slide from the plate on to the table-cloth, flipping over as it did so to reveal a little paper sticker, printed with the well-known logo of a frozen food firm, still adhering to its underside.

If, for whatever reason, you decide not to do the cooking yourself but to employ a chef, before you start to interview candidates you would be wise to have a clear idea of the type of cuisine you would like to offer and the level of excellence you aspire to.

Obviously, the higher the standard you hope to achieve

the more highly trained, experienced and over-paid your chef will need to be. What is perhaps not so well known outside the profession is that, unless you have the unlikely good fortune to happen upon a modest natural genius who is so happy among his pots and pans that he is unconcerned with material things, the more you pay your chef, the less control you are likely to have over him.

A top-flight chef expects to be precisely that — a chief: the undisputed head of a tribe of Indians whom he will insist upon nominating personally and ruling with absolute authority. Your rights in the matter are limited to paying their wages.

He will also expect a free hand in ordering the kitchen supplies — not only in the selection of the ingredients but also in the choice of suppliers. Those employers who are new to the game and its peculiar protocol, frequently find themselves paying over the odds for all manner of things, often for reasons that can most kindly be described as collaborative creative invoicing.

As a novice owner, a promising young chef who will co-operate with you, and progress with you, is much less likely to usurp your authority than an old hand who knows everything about running a restaurant, including the tricks of the trade that operate to his advantage and your deficit. Honesty is not a quality instantly associated with the catering trade — with some justification — possibly because of the difficulty of maintaining a tight control over stock which is easily disposable and, in the case of liquor, highly portable.

A really good chef, one who works in harmony with the proprietor and the rest of the staff, is a rare and precious possession and no one willingly lets one go. If you interview a chef who seems too good to be true, he probably is.

Curb your enthusiasm and find out precisely why he is looking for a new job; press him to tell you why he left his previous employment.

If his answer is: (a) because his employer died of a heart-attack and the restaurant closed down, or (b) because the place was burned to the ground by a fire that started elsewhere than in the kitchen, or (c) because he had a heart-attack and is looking for a somewhat less demanding job than his previous position as head chef at the Grosvenor House, then engage him on the spot. Any other reasons, however plausible, should be minutely and sceptically investigated.

Having decided on the kind of food you want your kitchen to produce, keep that firmly in mind in the course of your search. By all means be open-minded — even flexible — but don't jump at the golden opportunity that comes up unexpectedly without first making sure you have considered all its implications.

The charming Mexican, for example, with a host of intriguing Central American menu ideas, a folio of qualifications, a sheaf of glowing references and an affordable wage-requirement may seem like the very man to give your establishment an unusual cachet and a unique theme, but have you thought of the consequences should he fall ill, or be lured away by a better offer, or go beserk with the meat-cleaver? You could find yourself hastily substituting Thai curries, or roast beef and Yorkshire pudding for the Mexican menu you have been so energetically promoting, simply because he was the only Mexican chef in the whole of the eastern region and you have been obliged to replace him with a different breed of specialist. It matters little that the new man produces food which is as close to ambrosia as mortals can get — it is not what your customers have come for.

It is bad enough when a good chef leaves and his successor's *crème brulée* differs even slightly from that which your clientele have grown accustomed to; a major change in exotica is much more serious and will probably result in the mass defection of a fickle public.

Another sound piece of advice is never to 'poach' a chef from another establishment — if you can entice him away easily, others may be equally successful in luring him from you, probably on a bank holiday weekend.

An aspect of kitchen management which requires very careful consideration is waste — a catastrophic destroyer of profits. If you propose to serve roast sirloin of beef, carved from the bone at the table, you need to be pretty certain of the number of customers you can expect to be sitting waiting for it — or at least have a ready, and lucrative market for high-class roast beef sandwiches the following day. Should you, however, be relying on your advertising having reached its target in a properly persuasive manner, then your sirloin would be better cut into steaks and cooked as required, with that which remains unsold refrigerated for later use.

The catering business is a gamble — the trick is to learn the least risky number on which to place your stake. A spirit of adventure is a valuable quality in a restaurateur, but only if it is tempered with common-sense.

* * *

English is not, perhaps, the most felicitous language with which to describe food; too many of our culinary terms have unfortunate — or pessimistic — connotations. The dictionary definition of the word 'stew', for example, is better not gone into too closely on a full stomach, and the name 'string beans' must be the very nadir of mediocre expectations.

Nor are the Americanisms that have crept into our national cookery columns any better than our own self-conscious, and class-conscious homegrown terms. 'Starters', 'crispy, cheesy toppings', 'tangy sauces', 'jiffy bakes' and 'yummy sandwiches' (I quote) et cetera — surely we could do better than that?

The French have a happy knack of finding names and phrases which are acceptable to the entire nation. *Bonjour Monsieur* is a safe way of greeting any Frenchman whose name has escaped you, as is *Bonjour Madame* for a woman, whether married or single.

At the table they have a *plat principal*, preceded by soup, *hors d'oeuvres* or an *entrée*, and followed by *fromages* and *déssert*, in that order. Other ways of describing these do exist but no one will frown on you for using this simple formula whatever the circumstances.

In this country we don't even have universal agreement on what to call the meals themselves, much less the courses that constitute them. Lunch, dinner, supper, tea — they mean different things to different people. Writing your menu in French, with English subtitles, is one way of avoiding lining yourself up with any particular faction and also exonerates you from using that depressing word pudding in any other sense than its original one of a predominantly farinaceous preparation, sweet or savoury, which has been boiled, steamed or baked.

After all, since the publication of Nancy Mitford's 'U and non-U' exposé of the ins and outs of English upper-class vocabulary, loudly to demand 'What's for pudding?' no longer guarantees that one's formative years were spent in a draughty nursery under the auspices of a traditional English nanny, or that this early training was followed by a period of expensive privation at a fashionable public school.

Above all, whichever way you choose to write your menu, do avoid gushing superlatives like 'deliciously succulent lamb' and 'meltingly-tender fillet steaks garnished with divinely-crunchy baby haricots verts'. Such descriptions sound as false as they are ridiculous and are an open invitation to your customers to prove them to be a gross exaggeration. It is far better to keep your claims simple, honest and understated; if your lamb really is succulent the diner will discover the fact for himself in the eating, and be the more impressed by its excellence for not having had his scepticism aroused by spurious, flowery verbiage.

CHAPTER SIX

STAFF

Awaiting our dreamers in the harsh real world of catering is the reality of unending toil — something barely touched on in the pleasant sociable atmosphere of their dream. Their original resolve to do everything themselves until they get the hang of the business is rapidly waning. Of course they are going to need some help — but how much, and of what type, will depend on the size of their restaurant, the volume of trade they anticipate and the standard of food and service they propose to offer.

* * *

If you have arranged to take over a going concern the problem is simplified to some extent; you will already have an idea of the likely volume of trade and the approximate size of your overheads, and you may even inherit existing staff (but take care that this legacy does not include hefty redundancy entitlements). If not, you will be able to tell from the records how many were needed to maintain the level of business previously operating. This should permit you to keep the place ticking over steadily at least until you have found your feet and feel confident enough to make any changes — minor or sweeping — that you find necessary. If, on the other hand, you are starting up an entirely new business there are a great many things to be gone into before deciding the amount of help you will need.

If you are completely new to the restaurant business it may seem like a sensible policy to employ a trained professional who knows how things should be done, but unfortunately this does not always work in practice and you could find yourself being gently eased out of the control of your business.

For our first venture we took on the tenancy of a run-down country inn and in the early stages, apart from the daily contribution of a couple of cleaning-women, we did everything ourselves: serving in the dining-room and two bars, cooking and shopping, and any urgent cleaning jobs that needed doing in the afternoons and evenings and at weekends. (A mysterious and inflexible local custom, far more feared than the laws of the land which were occasionally treated with cavalier disregard, debarred the women of the locality from cleaning for money outside of the hours from nine a.m. to midday on weekdays only.)

It was desperately hard work but by the end of a year we not only had first-hand knowledge of every aspect of the business but had built up a clientele and gained a sound insight into the cost of running the place, so that the bills rarely managed to catch us unawares. By that time we were well placed to estimate by how much we could hope to increase our turnover with the help of extra employees and what, if any, percentage of these swollen profits would remain after the wages had been paid.

It is hardly necessary to mention that our carefully calculated decision to find a married couple to live in and carry the extra burden quickly translated into a medium-sized disaster. There was nothing wrong with the theory, but our judgement of character was horribly wide of the mark. On the face of it, employing people to do specific jobs at given hours for a stated remuneration seems straightforward enough and, in the case of a nine-to-five job in an office or shop no doubt it is. Catering is different.

Starting with the premise that two people — you and your partner — can serve an average of 120 *couverts* a week, it seems reasonable to assume that with the help of two extra people you will be able to serve at least twice that number. This may be the correct answer to the question as set in your ten-year-old's arithmetic text book but in the catering trade normal mathematical principles don't apply. It is well known, and understandable, that those who work for wages do it less hard, less long and less reliably than those who labour on their own account in their own business. Ask any doctor

35

how many self-employed patients visit his surgery regularly and he won't run out of fingers counting them up.

Because of this unfortunate fact of business life the increase in productivity brought about when you employ two extra pairs of hands is likely to be nearer to 60 per cent than 100 per cent. And the equation is still incomplete; as well as doing the same amount of work as before, you will have to spend time keeping track of the hours worked by your employees and monitoring their working conditions for any infringements of the Health and Safety Act (for their safety and your protection — from prosecution when they injure themselves by misusing the equipment). In addition you will find yourself working far into the night, calculating their wage entitlement in accordance with complicated rules covering overtime, split-shifts, double-time and holiday pay, and poring over PAYE tables until you are cross-eyed to establish the exact amount of the deductions you are required by law to make.

Then there is the monthly marathon session of filling in the endless, incomprehensible forms which constitute the returns you must send to the Inland Revenue on behalf of your employees — a particularly galling, unpaid chore, especially when you consider how much you are going to have to pay your accountant at the end of the year to do your own tax returns.

There is also a host of unexpected snags that can crop up when you have staff on the premises. These have their sources in various agencies but by far the majority of them can be laid at the door of the Health and Safety department.

The restaurant we ran for twenty-five years was well equipped with toilet facilities, both for customers and staff; there was even an outside lavatory for the convenience of the gardener. As long as we bumbled on doing all the work connected with food-handling ourselves and employing only part-time cleaners, the powers-that-be were content with our arrangements, or at least made no comment on them, but the day a waiter and a sous-chef were added to the payroll the seemingly innocent outdoor article of plumbing became a bone of contention between us and the health inspector.

It was a basic, old-fashioned, white porcelain affair with a wobbly wooden seat and a high-level cistern whose rusty iron chain had lost most of its white enamel handle, the whole enclosed in a cubicle of such meagre proportions that the addition of a lavatory brush and a tin of Harpic constituted overcrowding. It did not have the benefit of electricity laid on, which didn't matter, since nobody used it after dark. To us it seemed perfectly adequate for its purpose but the health inspector was of a different opinion.

'You'll have to install a wash-basin, with hot and cold running water, in there,' he told us 'with soap, towel and a nail-brush.' He refused to be drawn on the subject of how to fit it in.

'Only the gardener uses it, and he doesn't even eat here,' we protested.

'But if the other staff should use it they would have nowhere to wash their hands afterwards.'

'But they have their own toilet indoors — with lots of soap and towels, and nail-brushes.'

'But what if they did use it? It needs to be properly equipped, just in case.'

It was a ridiculous proposition; quite apart from the expense of laying on the electricity, installing a water-heating system and insulating everything to prevent frost damage in winter, there simply was no space to accommodate a basin and still be able to close the door.

For years the inspector included this complaint in his yearly report, classing it as top priority, but even he must have realized that he was on shaky ground, for he never pursued it to a conclusion. Eventually we tired of the game and, when the offending facility became leaky and in need of repair, we cut our losses and had it taken out, furnishing the delighted gardener with a built-in excuse for nipping off to the pub across the road at intervals throughout his working day.

* * *

When we started out, in the late 1950s, dining out for pleasure was not the universal leisure activity it is today, nor was the employment — or unemployment — situation in any way comparable.

In our country village none of the youngsters — whose experience of eating out was limited to the local fish-and-chip shop — would even consider a job in catering. Waiting at table equated in their minds with their grandparents' reminiscences of 'being in service'; girls thought it demeaning and preferred the nine-to-five chicken-plucking sessions at the poultry-processing factory, which left their evenings and weekends free. The boys, who were happy enough to wait on animals (and clean up after them) scoffed that cooking was women's work and waiting was a cissy job; they not only ran a mile at the mere suggestion but tormented the life out of any unfortunate youth desperate enough to give it a try.

Transport was a problem too, in those far-off days before car ownership became every countryman's right, and the area in which we could trawl for candidates was limited to a bicycle-ride radius.

Things are very different now; on the whole, it is an employers' market and an advertisement in the local press, or a card in the newsagent's window, should bring a good response — though not necessarily from the right calibre of people. Included in the replies you receive will be a number of applications for senior posts which were not mentioned in your advertisement; don't let this provoke you into accusing the newspaper of inaccurate copy — it is merely a manifestation of the optimism often displayed by the seriously under-qualified. You will be amazed how many prospective employees imagine they are being considered for your own job — and even more amazed that they could ever think themselves capable of doing it.

It is a useful idea to ask for written applications in the first instance and perhaps even to suggest that a photograph be included. Your customers will demand a certain level of standards from you and your staff and these are unlikely to stretch to an illiterate innumerate with slouching shoulders, a nose ring and a Mohican haircut, however charming his disposition. Weeding out such obviously unsuitable candidates at the earliest stage, rather than interviewing blind, will save time, expense (in reimbursing theoretical bus fares and even taxis) and frustration. Do remember to keep a representative selection of the more obvious works of blatantly collaborative fiction; they will brighten up your leisure hours in years to come.

Before you begin to interview the ones you judge to be worth a look, obtain and study copies of the welter of publications setting out employees' rights and employers' obligations (do not waste your time seeking for anything covering the reverse point of view — if employers have rights it would seem to be up to them to establish them without any help from government departments). Even the most illiterate know the contents of these documents by heart and will not hesitate to take advantage should you display ignorance of anything contained therein.

With this somewhat discouraging information at your fingertips you can proceed to make a list of the duties you will require your eventual employees to perform and work out a rough schedule of the hours when they will be needed. These should be flexible enough to fit in with the troughs and peaks of an unpredictable trade. It is also an excellent precaution against future strife to lay down strict house rules on such potential areas of contention as smoking, lounging about in the public areas and which parts of the premises (notably the bar) are out of bounds and to whom. Not forgetting minimum standards of dress.

It is far easier to relax rules which are too draconian than to toughen up a lax regime.

During each interview listen carefully to what the applicant has to offer. There are some who will turn down the job of trainee waiter or kitchen porter that you are moved by desperation to offer, despite strong reservations about their suitability for it, with a laconic 'Nah, I don't think so. Don't you need a barman (or receptionist, or under-manager)? I wouldn't mind doing that.'

Others may show a spark of enthusiasm and to these you should spell out precisely what the job entails, the degree of responsibility it carries and the measure of commitment it requires. Keep your options open, however, with a friendly warning that, when the business is under pressure (no need to say that this will be most of the time), they will be expected to help out with anything that needs doing. A small establishment certainly cannot afford demarcation lines.

If they are keen they should be prepared to come along for a couple of hours at a mutually convenient time, to give an unpaid demonstration of their ability — this is particularly illuminating in the case of kitchen helpers.

The hospitality business is notorious for seeking out slave labour and generally treating employees badly — a view unanimously subscribed to by mediocre staff and just about everyone outside the industry. It is both bad policy and false economy. Good employees deserve good conditions — bad ones you are better off without. This notwithstanding, when discussing remuneration leave room for manoeuvre; people's usefulness, productivity and adaptability vary enormously and it is helpful to be able to tailor the rewards to the results obtained — especially now that the Wage Council's statutory minimum rates have been rescinded and you no longer have to pay the same basic wages to all employees, regardless of ability.

Finding waiting staff can be a particularly frustrating experience. Even today this line of work is very low on the list of desirable life-time jobs and those who have chosen to make a career in it are usually well-suited with their present posts and can only be lured away at great expense. The majority of applicants will undoubtedly be women and fall into the following categories: (a) school-leavers who would really like a job on telly and, failing that, have no idea what kind of work they want to do; (b) those who have run out of credibility with the DHSS and need a job so badly that they will consider anything, even waitressing; (c) young mothers desperate to get out of the house and supplement the family income; (d) young women in further education attempting to bridge the gap between grant and reality.

The last two categories will almost certainly provide the most suitable candidates, if only because their manners are likely to be better, their way of speaking more appropriate and they have genuine, even laudable reasons for taking employment and won't consider the hours an unpardonable infringement on their social lives.

Unfortunately, drawing from these groups will result in a high turnover of staff; the perfect waitress is inevitably the one who, in two months' time, is destined receive a first-class honours degree and be off to the other end of the country, to start a brilliant career in a totally unrelated (and probably undeserving) industry.

Your desperate cry for daily cleaners and hourly washers-up (evenings) will probably bring down an avalanche of would-be head housekeepers. Forced to recognize the exact nature of the job you are offering these usually flounce off with the comment that they can get a job of that sort any time they like. Cleaners nowadays have high monetary expectations and aspire to grander titles.

By far your best bet — at any rate for the washing-up — is the little old dear from around the corner. Hard-working and gregarious, and full of good humour, if you are fortunate enough to secure one of these she is very likely to become the most valuable and conscientious member of your team. And, with a little luck, the busy evening clatter of pots and pans will drown out the steady stream of advice, gossip and reminiscences that originally drove her husband to encourage her to go out and find a job. In addition to her personal virtues she may also have a tribe of nieces and nephews, or grandchildren, who can be persuaded to fill in at the last minute, when your regular helpers are struck down by headaches, unsatisfactory love lives, nights out on the town or over-satisfactory love lives.

There are times when you will feel sadly disillusioned with the whole idea of employing staff; periods when they seem motivated by the misconception that you are in business solely for the purpose of providing them with a miserably inadequate wage at the end of the week, during which you are unreasonable enough to expect them to turn up regularly and go through the motions of earning it.

At other times you will think you have finally cracked it

and your organization is running like a finely-tuned Swiss chronometer. At this point you had better watch your back, just in case. Your perfect receptionist could already be four months pregnant and hastening you towards your first brush with the harsh realities of maternity leave; that super-efficient barman is probably even now conspiring with his girlfriend (your equally indispensable pastry-chef) to slip away at the first hint of spring and spend six months working for real money on a cruise liner, and the only really reliable cleaner you have could, against all the odds, come up on those football pools she is always popping out to post.

The path of the employer is hard, uncertain and rock-strewn, and the occasional primrose patch is no indication of smooth going ahead.

Even the law is heavily weighted in favour of the employee; catch one with his hand in the till and sack him on the spot in a rush of indignant moral certitude and you could find yourself paying him compensation for wrongful dismissal because you had failed to warn him (in writing) that larceny is not allowed on the premises and he must not do it again.

You, the employer, are legally constrained to give an employee × number of weeks' notice, calculated on his length of service, in order to terminate his employment. You may, and in most cases will, seek to limit the damage to that which has already been done, by paying him the wages involved and persuading him to go away immediately. He, on the other hand, can stomp out in a huff in the middle of a busy Saturday evening and still return next day to demand the balance of wages due.

The pregnant receptionist will be entitled to eighteen weeks of paid maternity leave — paid for initially by your good self — though with tenacity you may be able to claw much of it back. You are also obliged to hold the position open for her for twenty-nine weeks following the birth of the child, though she is permitted to wait until the very last moment of that period has expired before making up her mind whether or not to return. With the seven weeks she was statutorily absent before the event, this leaves you in limbo for a total of thirty-six weeks, during which period you will undoubtedly have had to bring in a replacement to keep your business from grinding to a halt. In your eyes this newcomer will be a temp but, in compliance with the law, you will none the less have to issue her with a contract of employment at the end of thirteen weeks, thus entitling her to all the benefits accruing to a regular employee — including maternity benefit.

Since the relevant qualifying period of employment is now reduced to six months, it is entirely within the bounds of possibility that the replacement could succumb to the same condition as her predecessor and set the whole tedious business in motion all over again.

During the years that we served among the ranks of catering staff employers, we did find a handful of gems; honest, conscientious people who enjoyed the work, tolerated the appalling hours and never failed willingly to put in that extra effort when the pressure was on. Despite our catalogue of dire prophesies they do exist — the trick is to find them.

CHAPTER SEVEN

CUSTOMERS — ALERTING THEM

Dreamers, like child psychologists, tend to imagine that people will react favourably to kind and fair treatment: that desirable clients are made, not born. It's an appealing theory but, in practice customers come in all shapes, sizes and temperaments; one or two of them are even on your side. These precious few are pearls beyond price and should be unfailingly cherished and cosseted. You can recognize them by the compliments they lavish on the food and service, their indulgent understanding when things don't go quite right and the unstinting way they sing your praises to their friends. Never, never make the mistake of neglecting them, even briefly, while you pander to the unreasonable demands of that unpleasant boor you suspect of being a food-guide inspector.

Unfortunately it is not practicable to select your customers according to suitability — particularly in the early stages of your venture. The type of cuisine you serve and your price structure will have been aimed at the sort of clientele you hope to attract, but only time, patience and hard work — and success — will empower you to pick and choose and weed out the less desirable elements.

Whatever their character or personality, the customers who have come to your restaurant are there because your food and/or ambience have been recommended to them — unless of course they were hungry and just happened to be nearby. If that recommendation came via a satisfied customer with whom they are on good terms they will already be predisposed to enjoy the fare that you offer and to give you the benefit of the doubt while they wait for it to arrive. If, on the other hand, they have been lured by the honeyed words of your advertising material, they will be waiting sceptically for you to back them up with deeds, and the more exaggerated the claims you have made for your wares the more uphill your task will be. It is worth bearing this in mind when framing your insertion in the press, or whatever medium you have chosen. Customers are a suspicious breed — conditioned, perhaps, by past disappointments.

Should you find that the economics of your operation cry out for large numbers of customers to be hauled in off the streets by any means possible, you will miss out on the precious personal recommendations provided by satisfied customers. Desperation and satisfaction rarely go hand in hand — which brings us back to the need to retain a financial cushion to sustain you through the early, difficult days.

Incidentally, if you start off as the tenant of a country pub, under no circumstances attempt to live up to the outstanding qualities of the previous incumbent, as described in glowing detail by the drinkers in the public bar. The simple act of moving on has automatically qualified him for canonization. No landlord was ever so liberal with drinks on the house, prizes (the bottled kind) for darts competitions or free food on match nights. Turn a deaf ear. Your turn to be similarly exalted will come, but you will no longer be there to witness it.

*   *   *

If yours is a completely new venture then your clientele will have to be attracted and built up, and there is no substitute in the early stages for getting out and meeting people. Make as much noise and as many contacts as possible during the period when you are building, converting or refurbishing; curiosity is a powerful magnet and if you can arouse it in potential clients you will have made a promising start.

If, like some dreamers, you can rely on a vast reservoir of friends and acquaintances to laud your efforts, that is a splendid help though the reality could fall short of your expectations; the most well-intentioned of friends sometimes need to be pushed into making the effort, and no matter how often they say to each other, 'We really must go and eat at Roz and Bill's place soon,' all too frequently it only translates into action when HE has forgotten THEIR anniversary and needs a last-minute table, complete with red carpet, to redeem himself. People are busy and there are a lot of distractions.

* * *

It is never safe to assume that you have the measure of new or potential customers and know how they will react in a given situation; they belong to an unpredictable species and are constantly finding new ways to surprise you.

An elderly, titled lady paid her first visit to our restaurant for the purpose of discussing plans for her granddaughter's engagement party over a light lunch. She went over everything down to the smallest detail; the food, wine, seating and flowers and, though she was meticulously correct, her manner had that touch of imperiousness indicative of a privileged background.

When all was arranged she paid her bill and P-J flung wide the front door to usher her out. To his horror, draped across the threshold was the unconscious form of a local devotee of Bacchus, temporarily deprived of his driving-licence by the magistrate, who had over-indulged his drinking habit at the nearby village pub and was sleeping off the effects of this lunch-time conviviality in the warm sun of the porch. The lady adjusted her spectacles and stood for a moment examining the recumbent man with wide-eyed curiosity, then a sweet smile spread across her face. Placing a hand on P-J's arm to steady herself, she stepped delicately over the body.

Her granddaughter's engagement party was hugely successful and the lady went on to become a valued customer, regularly bringing members of her large family to lunch or dine and never failing to inquire, with amused solicitude, after the well-being of her 'sleeping beauty'.

The opening of your new venture obviously needs to be trumpeted far and wide; the various methods of advertising are dealt with in the chapter dedicated to that subject, but it is worth noting here that, before splashing out on a full-page spread in the local newspaper to acquaint the neighbour-hood with your splendid new facility, it is a good idea to confer with those tradespeople who have had a hand in the fitting out, or who will be supplying your restaurant.

If the chap who installed the furniture and fittings is happy with the way they look *in situ*, he will fairly certainly be delighted to place an advertisement of his own in a box alongside yours, where he can boast that his work can be viewed to advantage by paying you a visit. Similarly the butcher, baker (and the candlestick-maker, if candlelight figures in your dream), not to mention the greengrocer, fishmonger and purveyor of fine cheese, should all be ready to profit from their association with the area's newest attraction. All their little boxes, strategically placed around your central feature, will not only add to its impact but substantially reduce its cost, since each will pay his share. And with a little luck, the editor of the paper, delighted with the advertising revenue, may even sanction a small article about your restaurant, yourselves and any interesting facts about either that you can supply him with — and all at no extra charge.

* * *

Appearance plays an important part in customers' first impressions and even if the exterior of the building is not specially attractive, it should be in good decorative order. The days of country properties mouldering away in picturesque decay are long gone and the humblest cottages nowadays are spruce and flower bedecked. This is probably because so many of them are now owned by refugees from the city rat-race, but no matter — if your restaurant is not in a presentable condition it will stick out like a whitlow on a thumb.

Appearance, of course, influences different people in different ways; the best features of our first restaurant — a handsome sixteenth-century inn — were concentrated at the rear of the building, overlooking the village churchyard: magnificent weathered-oak studs, infilled with soft, red, medieval bricks laid in a herringbone pattern, leaded casement windows and an overhanging first floor supported on fine carved beams. Except in the depths of winter, when they were just visible through the bare branches of the trees, it needed a dedicated effort, wading through knee-high nettles in the neglected graveyard, in order to admire these architectural gems.

The front of the house, from which all the doors, including the kitchen, opened on to the car park, had been encased in plaster many, many years before and, time having taken its toll, had reached the point where yet another cosmetic coat of paint did little to cover the cracks.

We kept the woodwork clean and smart, but we were tenants, on a yearly renewable contract; our landlords were not the owners either, and their lease was a trifle vague on the subject of repairs, so we petitioned in vain for a major face-lift.

Most of our clients sympathized with our dilemma and felt that the interior more than made up for the shortcomings of the outside but one or two were less forgiving. On one quiet, drizzly lunchtime in the early part of the year, we had only two small parties booked, one of which included a peer of the realm and the other a fringe member of the royal family. They all arrived dressed for casual anonymity and were quietly enjoying an aperitif in the bar when a brash commercial traveller breezed in and demanded a lager. He looked hopefully around for someone to sell something to and, finding only rebuffs, commented loudly, 'You'd get a better class of customer in here, you know, if you smartened the outside up a bit.'

* * *

Before the customer can admire — or criticize — your premises he first has to find them; easy enough if you occupy a prominent site in a well-signed village but less so if you have converted a remote farmhouse or mill. The directions offered by the indigenous population to tourists (a global term for anyone not speaking in the local dialect) are not always models of clarity and it is well worth fighting the inevitable protracted battle with the planning committee for permission to erect a sign at the turn-off from the main road.

A card showing a simple sketch map is also a useful addition to any publicity material you send out.

Assuming that your clients have found you and have not been put off by first impressions, the next hurdle is the entry to the premises. There are a surprising number of establishments — notably old country pubs — which give one no help at all in choosing between several undistinguished, and often identical, doors. On first visits we have wandered innocently into more than one kitchen, so do make sure that the door by which your clientele should enter the premises is clearly marked.

Your reception area is your welcome mat, and should be bright and cheerful; a poky, cramped entrance which forces customers to duck and dodge past each other or — worse still — keeps them waiting in the rain while a party of ten clutters up the doorway, making a leisurely, lingering departure, complete with multiple kissing of cheeks, is not the most auspicious opening to an evening of pleasure. It is possible to make up for poor first impressions but it is a terrible waste of energy and effort and much better avoided.

The most crucial of all impressions is the bright smile on the first face the guests encounter, be it that of Mine Host or the youngest trainee waiter — or even the charwoman, should you be so disorganized that she is still trailing the vacuum cleaner over the public area when the customers arrive. A smile creates a warmth that will stay with them while they wait for the barman to get his act together and serve them their drinks.

The bar, too, plays an important part in getting the occasion off on the right foot, so make sure that whoever is serving there knows what he is doing. The would-be James Bond who orders a dry martini will not take kindly to being served a glass of straight vermouth from a bottle labelled 'Martini Dry'. The established, classic cocktails should be known by heart but it is permissible to keep a little barman's bible under the counter to look up the more outlandish concoctions.

The pricing of your bar drinks needs careful judgement. This is one of the areas where the public is quick to complain of overcharging, usually behind your back, unfortunately, where no defence is possible. The legal requirement of standard measures of spirits makes it easy to compare prices with those charged in other bars. In itself, this is a relatively minor matter, but it will fuel the flames should there be cause for complaint in some other area. A trivial mistake which would otherwise have gone unnoticed could well go the rounds prefaced by such sour remarks as: 'Considering what they charge for drinks, they should . . . et cetera.'

If you have the time and facilities to provide a few good *canapés* with the aperitifs — like bite-sized *vol-au-vents*, tiny savory *tartelets* or half a quail-egg with mayonnaise on a cocktail biscuit (peanuts and crisps alone won't do) — your high bar prices will be justified in the eyes of the consumer.

A bar area with plenty of seating offers several advantages over a largely stand-up affair; people sitting in orderly groups around tables can study the menu in comfort and taking their orders is less prone to error than if they are milling around at the bar, where it is not always easy to be sure who belongs to which party. By all means distribute the menus as soon as the guests are settled, but avoid badgering them for an early decision unless they are in a hurry or you anticipate a rush later on. When the volume of trade is heavy it can be an advantage, and helps to relieve pressure on the kitchen, to leave those who are contentedly drinking in the bar until they tell you that they are ready to order. It's good for the bar trade, too.

It is essential for everyone who takes the orders for meals to be thoroughly conversant with all the dishes on the menu — not only how to pronounce them but roughly what they consist of, whether they are grilled, roasted, braised, baked or boiled, and what is served with them. It is extremely irritating for a customer to be obliged to interrupt the process of ordering while the waiter rushes (or saunters) off to the kitchen to ask whether the soup of the day is fish, vegetable or red herring. It is also a potential source of mistakes. Given too long to think about it, customers can change their minds or become confused about precisely what they have ordered. Even though the error was theirs, and not yours, if they finish up with steak when they are convinced they asked for salmon, they are not going to be happy.

The dining-room is the focal point of the whole operation, where your customers will spend the longest time and, no matter how good your food is, if they are not comfortable they will probably not come back. On holiday in Paris it may be fun to sit at those two-feet square tables, crammed together so tightly that only waiting staff far gone in anorexia can hope to move amongst them, but here at home they are more appropriate to a seaside café than a leisurely social evening.

Draw on your own experience as a customer here; forget, for a moment, the need to meet the bills and choose tables and chairs that are pleasing to you personally and arrange them in such a way that you would be content to spend two hours or more in any place in the room. This should not only ensure that your customers will be comfortable but should over-booking or some other dire necessity occur, will allow you to squeeze in a couple more tables at the last minute and still have room to make a reasonable stab at serving everybody correctly.

* * *

The party atmosphere often pictured by dreamers is delightful when it happens spontaneously because the customers all chance to be compatible, but it cannot be engineered — and certainly not by overcrowding the room.

Most of us enjoy meeting new people and exchanging views from time to time but it is something we must choose freely to do, not be forced into because the neighbouring table is so close that the alternative is to spend the evening talking in hushed tones and trying to avoid the eye contact that proximity makes inevitable.

Packing them in is sometimes tempting, especially when the phone suddenly comes insistently alive after a period of silence which had you thinking of renaming the place 'The Mary Celeste' but, unless you know the customers and you are reasonably sure that they will enter into the spirit of it, such a policy is rarely successful. And, if the strain it puts on the kitchen shows up in the results, you will soon hear unforgiving murmurings of discontent; all but your most partisan supporters harbour the suspicion that restaurateurs are congenitally a rapacious breed, greedily piling up money by any means at their disposal — particularly overcrowding and overcharging.

This slur on the collective character of what is, for the most part, an overworked and under-rewarded (at least monetarily) profession, is due largely to the general public's misconception about the cost of ingredients when purchased from a wholesaler. Ask a cross-section of restaurant-goers how much they think can be saved by buying fillet steak from a wholesale outlet, and the average of their answers would be around 50 per cent. The grim reality is that you will be lucky if you manage to get a 10 per cent reduction on the supermarket price. The same principle applies to a wide range of goods — generally speaking the higher the quality the less the saving to the restaurant buyer. So, as you struggle to hold your prices to a realistic level while still maintaining credibility with the taxman in the matter of your profit margins, the misinformed layman persists in his conviction that you are salting away a fortune on the strength of an extortionate mark-up.

Another strange notion we came across was the widely-held theory that, when a dish is described on the menu as containing cream, brandy or other lavish ingredients, it is actually produced, at virtually no cost, using cunning substitutes known only to caterers and kept jealously secret in the interests of inflating their already infamous profits. If these magical substances do exist we never discovered where to buy them.

A lady customer who was particularly fond of our *Poulet à la Crème* finally plucked up the courage to ask us for the recipe.

'No secret,' we told her, 'it's just the classic Normandy dish of chicken and mushrooms, poached gently in a sauce of butter and thick cream, thickened with egg yolks and finished with a glass of *calvados*.'

Her lip curled in a sneer. 'Anyone can do it with cream

and eggs,' she snapped indignantly, 'I hoped you were going to tell me what restaurants use.'

Returning to the subject of seating. If you need to re-arrange your tables to accommodate a large party, do be careful not to maroon a shy couple at a table in the corner, completely cut off from the rest of the dining-room by a table for ten or twelve. If the large party is convivial and even a little boisterous the couple will either feel neglected or overwhelmed; either way they are unlikely to enjoy them-selves and probably will never come back. As in many other walks of life, the things you get right will be noticed and appreciated only by a few perspicacious souls; the day something, no matter how trivial, goes wrong, everyone will notice.

Customers are flattered by the thoughtful host who re-members their names and such details as which table they prefer. It is worth keeping a dossier on your regulars and adding anyone who shows promise through the years, along with a record of their major likes and dislikes. When they celebrate a birthday or anniversary make a note of the date for future reference. If they come back the following year and you have had the forethought to provided a posy, or a small cake, it will be immensely appreciated and may set a precedent for years to come. People love to feel that they are special and their reactions to small courtesies are an enor-mous source of satisfaction to the restaurateur who enjoys his job. We used to keep track of our customers in a discreet red book that we kept firmly under lock and key in the office desk. The entries were given ratings from A1 to C4 — the letters denoting amiability of character and the figures spend-ing-power. One or two hard cases were consigned to a special category — SFH: 'Strictly from Hunger'.

One last, important feature of your premises must not be forgotten — the loos. Gone are the days when, as long as they were spotlessly clean, it mattered not that they were cold and draughty. A high standard of comfort — even luxury — is demanded now, especially on the distaff side. Good lighting, pretty vanitory units, mirrors that can be angled to give a view of the back of the hair as well as the face, and stacks and stacks of fresh towels — all these are indispensable. If your laundry bill is already a millstone around your bank balance and won't stretch to include huckaback or terry cloth, good quality paper towels are preferable to those tiresome hot-air machines which take forever to stew the hands to a clammy consistency, especially if you have lathered them properly and not just dangled your fingers briefly under the tap for the sake of appearances.

We knew of one restaurant that was famous far and wide. No one — at least not within our hearing — mentioned the quality of the food or the service it offered, nor yet the charm of its proprietors, but the magnificence of its marvellously-conserved, willow-patterned Victorian lavatory was fêted over three counties. Not that we are advocating a policy of clinging to past glories in the plumbing line — we mentioned the case only to emphasize the often quirky reactions of the restaurant-frequenting public.

One final word of advice on the subject of car parking. If it is at all possible, mark out your car park with spaces, or at least give some indication of the direction in which you would like the cars to line up. We had a car park which could comfortably accommodate twenty cars, sensibly placed, but on one notable occasion the first driver to arrive abandoned his vehicle diagonally across the very centre of the available space. The next two cars then painstakingly, though not particularly accurately, aligned themselves with the first and succeeded in using up all the space, so that that there was no room for anyone else. Life, today, is fraught with parking problems; unnecessary ones of that sort are the last straw.

CHAPTER EIGHT

OPENING

A very special opening menu or a free cocktail party are two of the ways of tackling the launch of your enterprise; there are others, but whichever you decide on there are a great many things to be organized first — notably stocking the kitchen and the bar. If you are the sole proprietors, with no ties to a brewery or other supplier you are free to contact all of the wine-merchants within your area, scrutinizing lists and discussing terms before settling on the one which offers the range of products you need, at the best price. You do not have to buy all your supplies from the same one, but such a policy could pay off in discounts for larger quantities.

If you can find a supplier who is willing to stock your cellar on a sale or return basis this is the very best deal of all, allowing you to keep a wide choice of wines without tying up large capital sums, but not surprisingly, this highly desirable arrangement is not offered to all, and may only come your way after your business is already well-established and thriving — and perhaps not even then. You can but try.

Price is not the only criterion to be considered; you may find it preferable to pay slightly more to a supplier who can deliver quickly and at short notice, rather than the cheapest one who only calls once a fortnight. Buying from the latter you will need to hold larger quantities on the premises — again tying up more capital.

To maintain a comprehensive list of wines it is essential to establish what stocks your supplier holds, or is certain of being able to obtain. There are few things more infuriating than taking delivery of your handsome, pristine new wine lists, fresh from the printer, only to find that, with the very next wine delivery, you have to cross out half the items and substitute something else. A good merchant should guarantee to hold an agreed amount of each line for you for a specified period.

For your kitchen supplies only experience will show you the best sources. It is worth seeking out good fresh poultry locally, rather than buying from catering wholesalers. It is surprising how difficult it can be to find plump, tender ducks with proper breast-bones, not cartilage that twists and shrivels during the cooking process, making them impossible to carve. The only way is to buy small quantities from different producers until you find a satisfactory product. Meat, too, can be tricky. The butcher who supplies the best beef does not necessarily sell equally good lamb or pork — we used to buy meat from two different local ones and have veal sent direct from London.

If your location is very rural and wholesale deliveries limited, a good retail greengrocer will provide the best vegetables and fruit, especially seasonal produce; or there may be a market garden near-by producing the organic vegetables which have such a strong appeal to the green-minded section of the public nowadays. You should be able to negotiate a reasonable discount and most traders are happy to obtain lines that they don't normally stock, provided you guarantee to take enough of them to cover their costs.

As to fish, supplies of this vary from one part of the country to another; if you are near the coast, buying direct from a port is a splendid plus, as long as you don't mind rising at the crack of dawn to go and bid for it. Apart from that, there are many excellent suppliers of fish to the catering trade and obtaining supplies should present no problem, especially as fish suffers less than most ingredients from deep-freezing, if it is super-fresh in the first place and properly handled during thawing.

Bread, too, is very important — we in this country have finally discovered that there are other kinds than the plastic slices we toast for breakfast or spread with butter (or some noxious alternative) at teatime. There is plenty of good, interesting bread to be bought nowadays — many super-markets make a creditable imitation of French baguettes with imported French flour. There are also some excellent part-baked products which need only a few minutes in the oven before serving; these are comparatively expensive but involve no waste as they can be cooked as required.

If you have the time and expertise, bread rolls made in your own kitchen are always appreciated, but do be gener-ous with them; too many establishments ration people to one grudging serving at the beginning of the meal; many customers will have acquired hitherto un-British bread-eating habits while travelling in Continental countries, where large basketfuls are left on the table and replenished as fast as they are emptied. Some people now also prefer bread to the dry biscuits that most restaurants still serve with cheese, so try not to make them feel they are being a nuisance, or keep them waiting while you bake some. It is far better to have some ready, even if it is wasted.

There are any number of firms who supply luxury ingredi-ents: frogs' legs, *écrevisses*, smoked salmon, eel and goose-breasts, *langoustines* and *foie gras* — almost everything is available at a price. When these luxury goods started flowing in from Europe in the early days of the Common Market, a small local firm which had supplied us with excellent poultry for some years, was taken over by a country-wide dealer in restaurant supplies. Suddenly their list blossomed with everything from *escargots* to Pacific prawns frozen in five-pound blocks, and — delight of delights — cryovac-packed *Magrets de Canard*, virtually unknown in this country in those far-off, innocent days before they were seized upon by the Art-on-a-Plate brigade. The elderly delivery man who brought our first consignment of *Magrets* handed over the package with a shake of the head and the bemused comment, 'Them's yer Margarets — whatever they are.'

He regarded the new range of products with marked distrust; delivering a gross of snails, along with our regular order of poultry, he checked the delivery note to be sure he wasn't mistaken. 'Snails? You buy snails?' He shrugged resignedly in the face of such folly and suggested hopefully,

'I could let you have some at a tenth of that price. My garden's full of 'em.' It was his unspoken opinion that we were out of our minds to pay good money for this outlandish foreign rubbish and that our customers should be certified for paying even more to come and eat it.

We are thoroughly spoiled nowadays in our choice of cheeses; almost all the glories of the French *fromageries* are available even in remote country areas. This was far from the case in the late 1950s and early 1960s, when the occasional underdeveloped Camembert that found its way on to our restaurant tables was cause for rejoicing. The tiny market town close by our first restaurant boasted a branch of a modest chain long since engulfed by some other grocery empire — and on our first visit we were delighted to find half-a-dozen Camemberts lined up on the counter. They were in good condition and we bought three.

The following week the remaining three cheeses, by then somewhat past their prime, were still there and the manager of the store was clearly disappointed when we declined them. They were there again on our third visit and on the fourth, at which point we inquired tentatively when he would be getting a new supply. He replied, with a steely glare, 'As soon as we've sold those.' They disappeared from the counter eventually — probably walking off of their own volition — but he never did get in any more. We used the store only rarely, once we were properly organized, but on one occasion we urgently needed something a little exotic in the way of canned fruit and asked the young counter assistant if they stocked lychees. The girl shook her head discouragingly and waved a limp paw in the direction of the dairy produce. 'Nah,' she said vaguely, 'only Cheddar.'

Cheese, incidentally, can result in costly waste; it is difficult to make an accurate estimate of your requirements and calculate your order accordingly. Depending on the probable quantities needed, you have the alternatives of ordering direct from a wholesale supplier or coming to an arrangement with the keeper of your local delicatessen. The latter will probably be happy to supply you at a price somewhere between wholesale and retail, especially if your order, added to his own, enables him to obtain larger discounts.

We used to buy the less perishable cheeses weekly from a wholesale supplier located about eighty miles away, and our order was delivered by Securicor. The first such delivery left us awaiting the bill with trepidation; could cheese really be so expensive as to justify armoured transport? The soft, perishable cheeses we bought as and when we needed them from the high-class grocer in the nearby market town. They cost more than from the wholesale source but saved us money in the long run, eliminating the need for over-buying and either throwing away the ones that went out of condition or leaving them on the cheeseboard long after they had ceased to be appealing.

Finally, a very useful source of many items is the cash and carry warehouse. There is bound to be one within a reasonable distance, wherever you are located. They are extremely convenient and competitively priced and an excellent source for dry goods, cleaning materials and basic canned items; they often have a good greengrocery section, too, and some also include a butchery.

You can see exactly what you are buying and take advantage of promotional offers, many of which are well worthwhile. If your head doesn't run to figures like £5.31 divided by 620 grams (decimalization, allied to totally unnecessary conversions, has left us with some extraordinarily inept quantifying) remember to take along a calculator, and never assume that the 'jumbo-sized catering pack' is the cheapest buy, but compare it first with case-lots of domestic packs. In our experience the latter are almost always more advantageous and also eliminate the trouble and waste of decanting the product into manageable containers before use. This applies particularly to detergents and other cleaning products.

If all this sounds rather petty and irrelevant to the main purpose of your enterprise, don't forget that, however much you enjoy your work and however high-minded your motives, your ultimate purpose is to make money — if only to keep your business afloat. You will be astonished how much of your budget can be eaten up by careless ordering and wasteful consumption of these non-productive items. To the housewife who comes daily to clean your premises, bulk packaging suggests an unlimited supply to be used with lavish abandon; this is all part of the widely-credited lore that businesses buy everything at a fraction of the price paid by the general public. If your cleaners work with the same kind of bottles and packets that they use at home, familiarity may just prompt them to use them sparingly.

*   *   *

Another heavy expense is your linen supply. The vogue for scrubbed deal tables with place mats is long past, and holidays abroad have conditioned customers to expect table-cloths and fabric napkins in any establishment that considers itself a cut above McDonald's. This can add up to a frightening quantity of laundry each week.

There are three main ways of appeasing your dining-room's appetite for clean linen. The first, easiest and least trouble, but by far the most expensive over a long period, is hiring. This entails virtually no initial outlay; you simply enter into a contract with the hire-firm to provide you with a stock of cloths, napkins, slip-cloths, et cetera, and arrange for them to call regularly to deliver fresh supplies and take away the soiled ones. An admirable, trouble-free arrangement — unless you count the trouble of covering the sizeable monthly cheque it entails — but the service is not always available in the depths of the country.

The second method is to buy your own linen and send it out to the local laundry. This is fine if you have a laundry conveniently to hand, but there are fewer of them than there used to be. The third, and probably your only option if your location is really a rural one, is to do the laundry on the premises, and for this you should buy the best modern machinery you can afford. Domestic machine cycles take too long to cope with the volume involved and commercial machines are ruinously expensive, but some manufacturers produce a mid-way range, suitable for small business like restaurants, guest-houses, old people's homes, and one of them may have something that will suit your requirements.

A tumble-dry facility is also a must — again for speed of operation — though if you have the space and the energy there is nothing to stop you from hanging the stuff on a washing-line in the garden on fine days (though not within sight of the restaurant; there are limits to what economy can achieve.) A rotary iron, or steam press, will also cut down on the labour costs of hand-ironing and make the job less appallingly tedious, when your laundress defects and you are obliged to do it yourself.

Incidentally, the snooper from the health department (or is that now the Department of Environmental Health? It's impossible to keep up with the ever-increasing self-importance of their titles) will throw a fit if you attempt to install your laundry equipment in the kitchen, no matter how large this is. A separate laundry room is a must, impractical and financially crippling though it be.

Real linen, if you can afford it (and find it) is infinitely easier and quicker to iron than pure cotton, which needs to start off much damper for a crisp finish. Linen also lasts much longer, which is just as well, since it is ruinously expensive. Possibly the best solution is cotton combined with synthetic fabrics; this is easier to iron than cotton alone and even wine-staining is no longer a problem for good modern detergents. So there we are — staffed, stocked, supplied and ready to go. All that remains is to decide on the path to take.

*　*　*

There are any number of opinions about the best way to tackle the actual opening of a restaurant: the day you await trembling and terrified, the verdict of the first customer to swallow the first mouthful of the first meal you produce professionally.

Some prefer the Grand Opening, announced well in advance, with incentives (usually free wine) and perhaps the promised presence of a celebrity or two if the proprietor has that kind of influence. Local reporters are wooed with complimentary meals and, in a properly ordered society and provided that the occasion is not a total disaster, respond with complimentary reports in their columns. Should you decide on this method you will be consumed by anxiety bordering on terror from the day of its inception until that blessed moment when, with a profound sigh of either relief or despair, you finally close the doors on a sea or, if you have been really unlucky, a trickle of departing backs. We would definitely not recommend this method to a complete beginner. Even for a seasoned operator it is fraught with peril.

To list all the things that can go wrong on these occasions would produce a small encyclopaedia. The equipment has not yet been tested under working conditions; the staff, unless this consists simply of the proprietor and partner, are not yet accustomed to working together as a team. The chef, no matter how experienced, will have to get used to the layout and uncover the idiosyncracies of his ovens, hobs and mixers (and no cooking equipment is completely free of these). If, in addition, the dining-room is filled to over-capacity, as usually happens, it is really asking too much for everything to go smoothly. And if you, the proprietor, are a total beginner, then the only recipe likely to be foolproof is the one for disaster. Of course, it is just possible your customers will make allowances and be understanding about the problems facing a new venture — but don't count on it.

Another popular method of getting a restaurant off to a flying start is a cocktail party before it actually opens. At such a gathering the establishment will be judged, not on its smooth-running efficiency but on the host's generosity with the liquor. It is appropriate only if you are hoping to appeal to a fairly 'chic' clientele, and you must be prepared to spend accordingly. Plonk and peanuts are, sadly, not going to place your prospective clients under a strong obligation to become paying customers. Modestly decent champagne and a good selection of *canapés* just might.

* * *

By far the safest course for the first-time restaurateur is to open his establishment quietly, preferably with the patronage of as many friends and well-disposed acquaintances as he can possibly muster.

The opening of a new restaurant always engenders a certain amount of curiosity and, with luck, this should bring in sufficient trade to carry you through your 'running-in' period, and give you and your team the chance to learn to work together, and put right any problems that occur, before you go on to more ambitious projects.

However carefully you have studied and planned your working layout there are bound to be adjustments to be made. Stations for cutlery, china and glass may need relocating; a door may open awkwardly and need rehanging the other way round, or a sideboard require moving a few inches or feet to left or right. Badly sited furniture and ill-defined 'traffic lanes' can cause hold-ups, breakages and friction: problems which will only show up in the course of serving real meals to real customers. Similarly, the staff may all have marvellous references and work extremely well individually but even the best of them need to get to know each other and learn to coordinate their efforts. There may also be personality clashes, which are often inexplicable, usually unpredictable and always troublesome. Only when the initial momentum begins to slacken and you feel you are ready to take on an increased workload, should you consider mounting a promotional event — even a grand opening, if you really must have one.

There is no law which requires the official opening night to be held on the very first occasion that a customer sits down to dine in the restaurant. Theatrical opening nights must, of necessity, be preceded by a period of rehearsal if they are to have any hope of being successful and there is no logical reason why caterers should not follow their example. Only rehearsals under working conditions that are realistic, without putting too much pressure on the untried team, will iron out these kinks in efficiency.

If you decide on a cocktail party, invitations need to be sent out far enough in advance to give those who have been properly brought up the time to respond. A handful of acceptances will boost your confidence during the last, nerve-racking hours as you set out glasses, chill bottles, put the finishing touches to the *canapés* and pray, genuflect, make the sign of the cross or prostrate yourself in an easterly direction, according to belief or preference.

Invitations should be sent to all professional people residing within the area, business people of standing, your wine-merchant, the vicar and anyone you can put a name to at the local press office and radio station. Not forgetting all your friends and acquaintances; even though you know they will patronize your restaurant anyway, you can't afford to offend them by leaving them out, and you'll probably be glad to have someone on your side.

There are a number of ways of compiling your guest list, the most long-winded and tedious being a laborious search through the telephone book and the Yellow Pages. The local Chamber of Commerce and such organizations as the Round Table may possibly offer some clues. It is useful, too, to drive slowly round the local industrial centre (even tiny market towns have them nowadays) noting down the names of the more prosperous-looking firms then checking for the names of the manager, directors, company secretary or whatever.

The advantage of the cocktail party over a grand opening dinner is the chance it gives you to meet and make an impression on your future customers. Use the opportunity to spend a little individual time with as many as you can, and have your bookings diary to hand in order to call the bluff of anyone who says 'We must come here to celebrate our wedding anniversary next month'. If only 25 per cent of those attending actually come back as customers in the following weeks, the exercise will have been worthwhile.

CHAPTER NINE

PUBLICITY

Advertising is a necessary evil; almost everyone has to use it at some time and, for it to be effective, it needs to be very carefully thought-out. A properly targeted campaign will help your business to expand and flourish but an ill-conceived one can be useless and even counter-productive. The finest publicity of all is the word-of-mouth recommendation of a satisfied customer, being completely free from the 'You'll have to do more than blow your own trumpet to convince ME' element inherent in the public's reaction to advertisements. Unfortunately, however freely given, this form of promotion rarely suffices by itself.

Next down on the quality scale comes the feature article in the press — preferably not linked to a paid entry. One that is fulsome in its praise is obviously the ideal but, should it turn out to be slightly critical, it will still bring you to the notice of the public; and if some of the customers that result from it are the unforgiving, 'Nobody-puts-one-over-on-me' type, their money is just as good as any other when it comes to paying the bills, and with tact and patience even those who come to mock can often be converted into regulars. This sort of unsolicited article can be diplomatically courted; journalists are constantly on the lookout for copy and, if you can think of a way of linking your business, your building or your person to some newsworthy incident or the anniversary of a notable event, a telephone call to the local paper could bring to your door a fresh-faced, eager young reporter, tape-recorder and camera in hand, anxious to immortalize you in his best prose and win his own byline in the process.

Before he arrives, decide precisely what you want to tell him and work out the best way to insert a few discreet plugs;

and make sure the interview is conducted in the most photo-genic corner of your premises, even if it does mean temporarily rearranging the furniture for the occasion. If you organize everything to your maximum advantage, not only can you cash in on that one occasion but you will probably make a useful ally of the writer for future projects. This approach does need discretion, though. The dining-out public is noto-riously cynical: quick to spot publicity that has been planted and suspect the restaurateur of bribery and corruption. Even if they, personally, have nothing against bribery or corruption they will not easily forgive you for trying to con them.

Paid advertisements come in various forms; the straight-forward entry in the local papers being the most common. In these one generally gives the name and location of the restaurant, the type of food served, the hours and days when it is open for business, the telephone number for bookings and — depending on your approach — an indica-tion of prices and even an implicit invitation to prospective clients to call you and your partner by your first names.

Before placing any advertisements it is advisable to study the various local newspapers and journals and judge which ones are most likely to have the type of readership you hope to target. According to how much you are prepared to spend, you can buy a single-column box, a full-page spread or anything in between. The small, regular entry is perhaps the most cost-effective; people with a sudden impulse to give cooking a miss and no established allegiances in the area, are more likely to leaf through the newspaper for ideas than to bother wading through the tortuous classifications in the Yellow Pages.

The full-page spread is useful at the outset to signal your arrival on the local scene and explain who and where you are and what you have to offer, but repeats of it should always have something new to say. Country newspapers have faithful readerships and any subsequent advertise-ments are unlikely to reach more than a handful of new readers, but the regular ones will almost certainly assume that, if you are wasting large sums of money on plugging the same old message, you must be doing badly. And sadly, human nature being what it is, there is little likelihood that they will be moved to rush out and patronize your establishment out of pure altruism.

*   *   *

From time to time newspapers and magazines will run a special feature about food generally or eating out in particular, and tout for advertisers to contribute to it. They usually offer special rates and the proposition should be looked at from all possible angles; sometimes, even though you may think there is little to be gained from the exercise, it can be detrimental not to join in.

Other ways of reminding the neighbourhood you are still there, ready and prepared to serve, include fly-sheets — single sheets of eye-catching paper printed with your message, which newsagents will, for a consideration, slip between the pages of the newspapers they send out. You can specify that they be included only with the type of paper likely to be read by the category of person you wish to reach.

Some of the unemployed, impecunious young can be paid to tour the car parks and tuck leaflets beneath the windscreen wipers of parked cars. Experience, however, has taught that a proportion of the aforementioned young, while anxious to receive the money, are less enthusiastic about earning it, so be prepared to find bundles of your precious printed matter dumped in the litter bin or abandoned behind the bushes in the park.

Distributing leaflets in your own immediate locality, where they will reach only those people who already know about you, has a slight flavour of desperation about it and it works better in appropriately affluent areas of the nearby town. It can, however, be particularly productive if you are situated in a busy tourist area, especially on days when it is raining just hard enough to dampen the visitors' enthusiasm for the great outdoors but not sufficiently to wash away the papers.

Business cards, attractively printed with the salient points you wish to get across, are useful items for 'planting'. The local tourist information office — most areas have one nowadays — will generally be willing to keep and distribute a small stock of them, and those of your suppliers who have retail outlets may agree to display a few in a prominent position for their customers to pick up. They do, after all, have a vested interest in seeing you prosper. With modern developments in computer and desk-top printing, such stationery items are easily and relatively cheaply produced.

* * *

Local theatres are another useful venue in which to advertise — they frequently sell space on their programmes and this is a particularly effective medium if you are in a position to cater for supper after the show. In fact, if you are clever in wording your entry (always keeping one eye on the Trade Descriptions Act) you could, without making specific claims, create the impression that your dining-room is the regular haunt of theatrical folk. The thought that they might be rubbing shoulders with the performers is a magnet for theatre-goers and a subtle suggestion that this is possible could easily turn into a self-fulfilling prophesy.

One form of publicity that is guaranteed to reach a very wide audience indeed is a mention in one of the guide books to eating in restaurants. Restaurateurs hold varying and individual opinions about this medium, which can be a blunt and uncontrollable instrument, and inclusion can provoke any one of a number of reactions, ranging from paroxysms of delight to abject despair.

The majority of these publications make no charge for the entries which are, at least in theory, unsolicitable, though a deluge of praise addressed to them by your friends and well-wishers would undoubtedly bring you to their notice; we know of people who have gone to considerable lengths to engineer this introduction, even writing the letters themselves and persuading their more compliant customers to sign and post them.

It is not a good idea to telephone the editors yourself, however innocently, to indicate that you are ready and willing to be investigated; the howls of moral indignation and protests of incorruptibility resulting from such an imprudent approach could seriously compromise your future inclusion. In your dealings with guide books, as in more personal relationships, if there is mutual respect the partnership will be harmonious and beneficial. It is not unknown, however, for contributing journalists to put good copy above accurate reporting and even when restaurateurs have cooperated fully and filled in endless questionnaires, the resulting entries are not always 100 per cent accurate; some of the ones that were written about our restaurant were misleading and a few even bordered on malevolence.

The primary objective of these books is, presumably, to help travellers to make an informed choice of where to eat in an unfamiliar region, but they also influence people living nearby. If your establishment is described in glowing terms in a newly published edition, a proportion of local people who have never been before will desert their regular haunts to come and see why, and while initially, of course, it is good news, it can be a mixed blessing. You will be deluged with bookings for a week or two following publication — and the attendant reviews in the food and drink columns of the newspapers — and your till will be ringing merrily. Unfortunately, it will also result in strained relations with those of your regular customers who, in consequence, have difficulty in getting a table. Once the fuss and the lionizing has died down, you may find to your cost that your restaurant had acquired a reputation for always being fully booked and not worth the cost of a phone call at less than a month's notice. Wonderful for as long as it is true.

On several occasions regular customers, phoning to make a reservation, remarked, 'We almost didn't dare ring. After that wonderful write-up we thought you'd want much more notice.'

'That was more than a month ago,' we would reply, ruefully surveying our half-empty dining-room.

We spent twenty-five of our thirty years in the business, in a state of conflict with one or other of these guides. Like the Hundred Years' War it was an affair of lulls and skirmishes, and periodic pitched battles. In our opinion, they concerned themselves too little with the quality of the food, and dedicated too much space to the deficiencies of the décor, the idiosyncracies of the staff and the personality of the owner. This made amusing reading for those not directly involved but had small bearing on their avowed purpose to inform. They made very few criticisms of our food — and almost all of those were either trivial or ill-informed — but the snide style of writing gave ammunition to certain types of customer who had no interest in what they were eating but took perverse pleasure in trying to goad us into tearing up the bill and asking them to leave before they had quite finished their expensive meal.

We are not suggesting that you should become suicidal the moment your establishment makes its début in a food guide, nor even that you will necessarily be dissatisfied or upset by what is said about you. It is possible that you will be delighted both with your entry and the results it brings. It could be overwhelmingly complimentary and bring to your door customers who are charming, appreciative and generous. But if not, at least you now know that you are not the first to fall foul of the system.

* * *

Some years ago a competitor in our area actually indulged in a thirty-second burst of publicity on local television but, as an advertising medium, television is nowadays largely beyond the reach of small businesses.

A telephone call to our local independent radio station, which serves an area populated by around half a million adults, brought us a glossy brochure containing their up-to-date audience statistics and a graph of their charges, as applied to the different times of the day.

There is no doubt that radio advertising is extremely effective; an equally glossy pull-out tells of the campaign, launched well in advance of the opening of a new shopping complex in their home city, which resulted in large numbers of potential customers rushing to the site months before the shops had even begun trading. Whether or not it would be as effective in your case is another matter entirely. A thirty-second spot of air time is an ephemeral thing — lost forever the moment it is completed. The success of this medium depends heavily on repetition of the message, which inevitably increases the expense.

The basic price chart is clear enough for the purpose of initial assessment but, with its multiple codicils of surcharges, discounts and percentages for greater or lesser durations, should you decided to give it a try you might need the help of a trained mathematician to work out what you were letting yourself in for — though the charming young woman who answered my call did invite me to contact her again for help or further information.

The price structure, calculated in time segments set against availability levels, boils down to higher charges for those times of the day when people are driving to and from work, or ferrying the children between home and school, reducing to the lowest amount between the hours of six p.m. and midnight — the time when the very people you hope to influence are probably dining, if not at your restaurant then somebody else's. The cost of a thirty-second spot ranges from the price of a modest lunch in a decent restaurant to that of a weekend break in a three-star hotel and you must draw your own conclusions about its cost-effectiveness in your particular case.

* * *

Advertising, like all branches of expenditure, needs to be judiciously targeted to achieve the best results. It is obvious that, to be effective, entries must be placed in those publications likely to be read by the people you wish to attract, but timing is also important. If your weekends and holiday periods are already well-attended, then an advertisement that increases your overall trade is misdirected. You must devise a campaign that specifically seeks to fill the empty tables on slack evenings, rather than indiscriminately attracting greater numbers, most of whom will probably want to come at the weekend anyway; otherwise we come back to the 'always booked up' syndrome.

In that blissful restaurant heaven, where all deserving caterers will surely spend a rewarding eternity, custom will be spread evenly over every day of the week. Were it possible to achieve this happy state here on earth it would give an undreamed-of boost to your receipts and a priceless gift of insight when working out staffing-levels — that bedevilled aspect of administration governed by mysterious cosmic laws that keep waiters hanging around for hours, doing quite the wrong kind of waiting, and then usher in crowds of casual callers the moment you have cut your losses and sent most of them home. The fight to redress these natural imbalances is unending.

If you buy a going concern, rather than converting and equipping new premises, you will have the advantage of starting off with a ready-made customer base — at least for one visit each. Prudent restaurateurs keep a mailing list of all worthwhile customers and send out details of attractions they are preparing; it is also a good policy to have 'house' Christmas cards printed and send them to as many clients as possible. Some of those will miss the point and send you a card in return, but a proportion should get the message and include your establishment in their festive plans.

During the protracted negotiations surrounding the purchase, you should have requested that this list be passed on to you as part of the goodwill. It will be useful for targeting suggestible people when trade is stuck in the doldrums and you are trying to drum up support for a St Valentine's Day party or a Burns' Night supper.

As long as you explain that you will be using them to give advance warning of special functions, customers are generally happy to leave their names and addresses (assuming they have enjoyed their visit) unless, of course, they happen to be called Mr and Mrs . . . Smith. Never press the point if they show the slightest reluctance.

Finally, don't forget that your own attitude towards what you are doing can be infectious. If you are genuinely interested in food and justifiably proud of that which comes out of your kitchen, your enthusiasm is bound to rub off on your customers.

Small restaurants in Paris, and all over provincial France, have a notice board, prominently displayed near the door, proudly boasting: *LE PATRON MANGE ICI!*

CHAPTER TEN

GIMMICKS AND ATTRACTIONS

'Things are going fine — we've attracted plenty of the right sort of customer; now we should think seriously of ways to keep them coming back.'

'That's easy; give them fabulous food and prompt, friendly service.'

'That's all very well but a business is not a time capsule. It's got to keep moving forward. New ideas — gimmicks.'

'What a horrible thought! What do you suggest? Paper hats? House wine at half price on slack Thursdays?'

The dreamers are arguing unnecessarily; they are both partly right and their differences are not irreconcilable. She is convinced that, having found a successful formula, the slightest change would prove damaging, and in some cases this is so. He, on the other hand, has learned that in business, you cannot stand still; if you don't go forward you must inevitably slide back. This view too, has a lot going for it.

Inflation is now an established part of modern economics, and rising overheads demand a corresponding increase in turnover — unfortunately only achievable by putting up prices, attracting more custom, or a combination of the two. When customers come year after year to eat the same food in the same dining-room, among the same number of fellow diners, they will eventually wake up to the fact that the meal which cost them £10 a head five years before now sets them back £25 or more — a greater increase than that which they have noticed in their domestic food bills.

The reason for the discrepancy does not, as they immediately conclude, lie in greed and overcharging, but in increased wage and fuel costs, and all the other out-goings which come into the calculation.

People with no commercial experience are inclined to view the question of pricing in simplistic terms and it would be a thankless task to try and convince them that putting 5 per cent on the price of a steak does not adequately compensate for a 5 per cent increase in the cost of beef.

A couple of regular customers came to dine at our restaurant once a month and their choice from the menu never varied: Pacific prawns in mayonnaise, with a half-bottle of *Pouilly Fumé*, followed by a thick *entrecôte* steak in a *Bordelaise* sauce and a half of *Côtes de Beaune*. They stoutly maintained that they had never eaten the equal of these dishes anywhere and steadfastly refused to risk disappointment by trying something else.

The Pacific prawns, which weighed around two ounces each, were supplied deep-frozen and arrived in solid, five-pound blocks which, if dropped from a great height on to a concrete floor, would shatter into forty or so ice-jacketed, individual fish. At that time — 1960 — they cost three shillings and sixpence per pound and we charged a little more than twice that for a portion. They were one of our best-selling lines. Then one day when we telephoned our weekly order we were told that they were no longer available.

Our two customers were inconsolable. They tried *pâté*, salmon *quenelles*, scallops, but nothing compared with their favourite prawns and, eventually, they simply stayed away. For several months we heard nothing more from them.

Then the Pacific prawns became available once more, but with a huge price rise which put them on our table at eighteen shillings and sixpence — the same as the *entrecôte* steak.

We telephoned our prawn addicts and told them the glad tidings mentioning, without dwelling upon, the inflationary effect that absence had wrought and they booked there and then for the following Saturday.

It was touching to watch them tuck in to their favourite dish, and even the steak which followed it was, they assured us, the tenderest they had ever eaten. In fact, their mood was so expansive that they actually ordered an unprecedented extra half-bottle of red wine. It was a nostalgic evening; we had missed their regular visits and they confessed that life had not been the same for them either. The prodigals had returned.

But even a perfect evening has to end and shortly after midnight they called for the bill. Unbelieving, we added up the items three times before writing in the staggering total; apart from the high price of the prawns, the Chancellor of the Exchequer had recently announced his budget and the pound of flesh that he levied on the wine, plus the extra half-bottle, and a seasonal increase in the cost of beef, all combined to produce a final sum *almost twice that of previous occasions.*

La douloureuse, true to its name, caused the customer considerable pain — not to mention anguish. The man abandoned his established custom of adding a modest gratuity and wrote his cheque in the exact amount, to the very last penny then, after a cursory leave-taking, they walked out into the night, backs bristling with unspoken indignation; we never saw them again.

We took the lesson to heart and warned the other customers that the prawns were now ruinously expensive; most of them bridled slightly, resenting the implication, and paid their bills with a scarcely perceptible 'ouch'. Soon the dish was back on the best-selling list and we were moving on to our next lesson in psychology.

It was not long in coming, delivered this time by a charming, friendly couple who also came regularly, about once a month. He was a gruff bear of a man and his wife petite and pretty. They enjoyed their food immensely and particularly loved the sorbets, ice-creams, *soufflées, meringues* and other delicate offerings that came at the end of the meal, but every time, after making their choice, the husband made the remark: 'You really should serve proper English puddings, you know, instead of this airy-fairy stuff. Spotted Dick, now — that's my favourite. Good rib-sticking suet-pud with lashings of lumpy custard.' He was teasing us, of course and one day we thought it would be fun to tease him in turn.

For their next visit, the chef baked a thin, light sponge, liberally studded with raisins, and made it into a convincing facsimile of a suet pudding by wrapping it around a cylindrical core of Grand Marnier flavoured ice-cream — one of the wife's favourites.

We sent this to the table on a silver salver, together with a large jug of rich *crème Anglaise* — lumps represented by bits of crushed meringue — and the effect spoiled only marginally by the steam, which dropped downwards instead of rising.

'The chef has made a traditional pudding, especially for you, sir,' said the waiter with a flourish. The man went pale, clutched at his throat and croaked, 'Spotted Dick! You didn't!' The wife leapt to her feet and menaced him with divorce.

Eventually they laughed at the joke and settled down to demolish, and thoroughly enjoy, their pudding but, despite that, we found subsequently that we had badly misjudged their reaction. They came a few more times but the traditional 'Spotted Dick' pleasantry had been laid to rest and we got the distinct impression that they felt we had overstepped the mark. Their visits became more widely spaced and finally tailed off altogether; we never again permitted ourselves to lose sight of the sobering fact that, however friendly clients appear to be, you must always be prepared for them to revert to customer status at the drop of a fork.

* * *

Once the excitement of the opening has died down and your establishment no longer has the advantage of novelty value, there are a number of questions you should ask yourself about the direction in which your business is going. What sort of clientele have you succeeded in building up? How many of them come back regularly? Is there a good influx of new customers? Is the overall volume of trade adequate? And if not, what can you do about it?

Unless you have miscalculated your financial requirements and been forced to adopt a 'drag 'em in at all costs' policy in order to cover your overheads, the bulk of your clientele will most probably consist of the kind of people you originally set out to attract. Those who do not measure up can be discouraged by small adjustments, like temporarily dropping their favourite items from the menu, or imposing a minimum charge (which can be waived at your discretion). Small rebuffs, if they are administered with scrupulous courtesy, can be very effective.

Several years of living in Italy before starting in business had conditioned us to expect a plate of pasta to be followed by a substantial meat dish, and we naturally put *Spaghetti Bolognese* on our menu among the first courses, priced accordingly. Before long we found, to our irritation, that a number of customers had taken to coming several times a week to eat a dish of *Spaghetti Bolognese*, without even so much as a glass of wine to help to cover the cost of the linen and service. The practice had to be discouraged — the spaghetti-eaters were occupying tables that could have been put to better use and, with our overheads, we were definitely not interested in running a quick-lunch counter so we transferred the dish to the main course category, at double the price for exactly the same quantity. This had the desired effect; the offenders squealed indignantly and went elsewhere and those among our proper customers who wished to eat pasta as a first course considered themselves favoured to do so at half the stated price.

Your good regular customers are the barometer of your success. The ones who keep coming back for more not only form the bread-and-butter of your business but can be counted on to proselytize on your behalf wherever the subject of eating out crops up. It is well worth the trouble of rolling out the red carpet whenever they visit and if there are days when you simply don't have the time to give them the accustomed preferential treatment, at least try to make them feel that you would if you weren't run off your feet. Customers, like lovers, can become jealous of small prerogatives — giving THEIR table to a complete newcomer or failing to make the opportunity to chat with them because a visitor from foreign parts is claiming your attention.

There will be times of the year when your regular trade drops away and your bank balance shows symptoms of severe anaemia but, before setting up the apparatus for a transfusion of new business, you must be certain that the group to which the fresh supply belongs is compatible with that already flowing through your commercial veins. Hosting the rugby club annual dinner may bring a welcome flush to your bank manager's cheek but, if your regular customers fall into the sedate, middle-class, middle-aged, middle-income category, it is more likely to contribute to the decline of your business than to herald a new era of robust health. It is far better to try and awaken the flagging interest of existing customers by organizing a special occasion that will both appeal to them and, with luck, attract like-minded newcomers to share in it.

A special evening dedicated to the cuisine of a particular region is one example: perhaps the famous specialities of Burgundy accompanied by Burgundy wines. It is tactful to offer places at these special occasions first to your established clientele through your mailing-list, well in advance of the date, and leave information cards conspicuously on the tables or tucked into the corner of your menus. Once you have evaluated their response you can then advertise in the local press, if necessary, to supplement the attendance. If you are encouraged by the response to the first of these promotions, you could go on to propose a series of such evenings, devoted to other regions or countries and perhaps publish a calendar of them. We found that people who met at one such occasion frequently got together as a group to attend a subsequent one — making a party of it. Sometimes customers will suggest a theme themselves. One dismal winter evening in the aftermath of Christmas, we were persuaded — in the teeth of opposition from the kitchen staff — to hold a Burns' Night supper.

Happily for the eardrums of those ensconced beneath the low, heavily-beamed ceiling of our dining-room, no piper was available in the rural depths of East Anglia. The traditional recipes, too, underwent a few subtle changes in their passage through our kitchen: the cock-a-leekie soup had a strong French accent (the mandatory prunes were served as an optional extra): the salmon, while admittedly caught far to the north of Hadrian's inadequate barrier, was smothered in Hollandaise sauce made with purest Normandy butter.

The first sight of the haggis, as delivered (our dictionary offers neither gender nor plural for this uncharismatic creature) sent the chef's hands skyward in a gesture of despair, but they eventually graced the festive board upon a long silver platter, dressed for the occasion in mantles of pheasant plumage normally used to decorate galantines, their sallow complexion hidden beneath the feathers, sporting three birds' feet apiece to maintain a precarious balance and a sprig of white heather in their uplifted beaks. Their entry provoked a burst of spontaneous applause from the assembled company which, in all honesty, did not include a single genuine Scot. The root vegetables the cookery book insisted were the proper accompaniment, had been enriched with enough butter to fur up the arteries of an entire Highland clan.

We served oat cakes, in expensive tartan packaging, with the cheese, and exploited the traditional link between France and Scotland to justify piling the cheeseboard with goodies of distinctly un-Caledonian provenance.

The meal ended with shortbread, made by the chef with even more Normandy butter, and a dish of Atholbrose (according to the only description we could find, a combination of unspecified quantities of cream, honey and Scotch whisky) that was strictly off-limits to those unfortunates delegated to drive home. The evening was such a resounding success that it became a popular fixture in our calendar of events though, fearing reprisals, anyone who knew more than two stanzas of Burns' poetry by heart was firmly discouraged from attending.

* * *

There still exist, we are informed, establishments where the arrival of the *Beaujolais Nouveau* is deemed cause for celebration, though we suspect that this tradition — of recent manufacture — is destined for early extinction. The fact that it came into being at all — much less enjoyed such notoriety — must be a source of encouragement to anyone who imagines he has invented a new gimmick to pull in the punters.

The average Frenchman has a lasting regard for his country's mores, particularly those concerned with his stomach, and he will treat with peculiar respect anything which can lay claim to being rooted in French culinary history, whether or not it is palatable to him personally.

Beaujolais Nouveau, like *Andouille* — a deplorably unappealing offal sausage, made by stuffing a pig's large intestine with smaller intestines in ever-decreasing concentric layers — falls within the category of items which he will dutifully consume once a year, in the firm, if misguided belief that all traditions are worth preserving. The ingenious Frenchman who conceived the notion of foisting off a substantial proportion of the stuff on the unsuspecting English restaurant-goer, must command our profound admiration.

A less specious way of using wine as a theme for a promotional evening is to organize a wine-tasting in collaboration with your wine-merchant. Most good wine-suppliers are happy to provide an expert to conduct the actual tasting and, as long as you have no objection to his bringing along order forms and encouraging the tasters to buy case-lots of those products that they find most appealing, he will probably furnish the wine for tasting free of charge.

You will need a large table on which to set up the wines and must provide plenty of glasses (and a team of waiters and washers-up to keep the supply coming) and some simple finger-snacks. It is as well to consult with your expert in advance on the form that these should take — some wine buffs hold strong views on what is and is not appropriate to the tasting process. But don't allow yourself to be bullied into offering anything more than dry crusts; you want the customers to be impressed with your contribution, as well as with the wines. Spittoons are rarely required at such gatherings these days but it is as well to have some sort of receptacle available for the odd purist and/or show-off.

The event usually takes the form of an illustrated lecture — the illustrations being poured sparingly into glasses to be admired, sniffed, tasted, compared, talked about and ultimately ordered, by suitably edified customers, in case-lots specially discounted for the occasion. This takes care of the merchant's profit on the evening's work.

We invariably rounded off the evening by hastily putting the dining-room back together again and offering a simple meal with a limited choice of dishes; after tasting a dozen or more wines and nibbling the snacks we provided as blotting-paper, no one felt up to eating a full meal.

As to financing the evening, one policy is to issue invitations to the tasting and make a charge only for the meal which follows. You face the possibility that a few of the guests will taste and run, but there should be enough active social consciences present to make the evening a success. Another way is to sell tickets at a price which covers the tasting and the subsequent meal, including a choice of the wines they have sampled. A gathering of this type helps to promote social mingling among those who attend — a very desirable outcome. Customers who know and like each other make for a friendly, relaxed ambience which is far more pleasant than a stiff, formal collection of individual parties conversing conspiratorially amongst themselves.

* * *

Change is a double-edged weapon; some customers resent change of any sort. Every dish on your menu is bound to be somebody's favourite so that whenever you decide to drop one it will cause disappointment to someone; alterations should never be too radical unless you envisage a wholesale shift of policy and a complete change in the type of clientele. By all means offer *nouveautés* but monitor customer reaction to them carefully. It is regrettable, in some respects, that modern distribution methods mean the seasons no longer play much part in dictating what we eat. There was a time when supplies were governed by the calendar and no one expected to eat strawberries in December — or new potatoes, for that matter.

If you feel that a radical change is the only way of revitalizing your business then we recommend that you make a feature of it. Advertise your intentions; close for a few days, perhaps, and change the decor — or at least move the furniture around — cross your fingers and hope that your customers will feel that you are creating something new and exciting rather than just tinkering with, and in some opinions spoiling, the established order. Whatever you do is bound to upset someone, and probably for some obscure reason you can't begin to understand.

The well-known aphorism, ascribed variously and inaccurately to Henry Ford, Sam Goldwyn and others, encapsulates the difficulty of pleasing all of the people all of the time; as a restaurateur the most you can hope for is to placate as many as possible for most of the time.

CHAPTER ELEVEN

RUNNING IT SUCCESSFULLY

'We've worked like slaves for a year and everything is running like clockwork; don't you think it's time to get in some staff and sit back and enjoy it? Perhaps even take a break?'

'Sounds like a good idea. A chef and a working manager — that's what we need.'

We have all been through this stage, when we trustingly believed that we could unload the burden of the daily grind and sit back and let hired help take the strain. Despite a lurking suspicion that anyone competent enough to run their business has probably already set up one of his own, dreamers do tend to cling to the illusion that the boring part of the work can be delegated to employees. Unfortunately, even if they did find the ideal team to run their business for them, they would have to pay generous salaries to keep them — and keep them honest — and probably a share of the profits as well. Frankly, most country hostelries simply don't make enough money to warrant such an arrangement and the majority of proprietors resign themselves to a life of hands-on management.

There are times when the restaurateur's job resembles that circus act where the performer balances spinning plates on sticks set up around the ring, and then circulates frenetically among them, keeping them all rotating fast enough to prevent them from falling.

Before leaving your business in the care of employees for a few days, you will have to set all your plates (figurative, not actual) whirling at such a furious pace that even the restrained enthusiasm of your staff will be enough to keep them rotating until you get back. Sadly, you will find that you are the only one who really cares if the occasional one winds down and crashes to the floor and your second job when you return — after you have got the plates spinning again — will be to pick up the pieces and glue what you can back together.

Some couples take separate breaks and holidays, so that one of them is always there and in charge. They are the ones who feel that working together, day in and day out, is togetherness enough and welcome the chance to spend their leisure time apart; for them this is an admirable solution. There are others who would be appalled at the prospect. It's all a matter of temperament. The right solution for you will turn up sooner or later and allow you to take the breaks and all the other perks that are necessary to make the job bearable, so let's forget all about early retirement, holidays and the good life in general and get down to the serious business of the long-term management of that restaurant you always dreamed of running.

* * *

The day-to-day running needs to be based on strict routine, tempered with enough flexibility and adaptability to allow you to cope when life throws a spanner in the works — rarely less than a dozen times a week, on average. The best of staff are the schizophrenic ones who are always completely reliable as far as their work is concerned, but have absolutely no compunction in letting down their family, friends and team-mates on a regular basis whenever the business goes haywire and you need them to put in extra hours at little or no notice. Not surprisingly, these paragons of selective loyalty are rare. We have long been amazed that anyone should actually choose to do a job that requires them to work when the rest of the world is playing, or at least resting, but fortunately there are still some who do, and some of them even do it well. Until you succeed in finding your personal quota of these models of probity, you must resign yourself to making up with quantity what the ones you can get lack in quality.

Good business practices are essential to success, and perhaps the most important one is the keeping of sound financial records. If you are new to business this cannot be stressed too often or too strongly. You must be aware of the exact amount of money that passes through your till and precisely where it all goes to. Quite apart from being very much in your own best interests, both the Inland Revenue and Customs and Excise will take a keen interest in this aspect of your affairs — the former in order to extract the maximum possible tax on your profits and the latter to ensure that every penny of the VAT they have obliged you to extract from a reluctant general public is properly passed on. However handy it may be, it is unwise to borrow even small amounts from the till for your own purposes. It shows a bad example to the staff and, should you forget to pay it back, leads to approximate reckonings which, at best, will obscure your profit margins. Your business is not a direct extension of your wallet.

Our forebear who owned the pub surrounded by airfields told us about his RAF officer customers, who used to confide in him that, on leaving the service, they planned to keep a pub.

'And that is precisely what most of them will finish up doing,' he said, ruefully. 'I try to tell them that the pub is there to keep them, but it can only do so if it is properly run, with hard work over long hours. They see it just as a sociable occupation — a sort of civilian version of the officers' mess.'

* * *

Apart from the ability to organize and motivate staff and keep accounts conscientiously, there are a number of personal qualities which can smooth the path of the restaurateur fortunate enough to possess them.

Patience is a must, especially when dealing with customers who cannot make up their minds, or those who keep you hanging about late at night, long after they have no further intention of contributing to your day's takings, and the ones with an unerring instinct for the worst possible moment to order your most labour-intensive dish.

Tolerance is another precious gift which will serve you when you are dog-tired and stone-cold sober, and condemned to watch your well-wined clients acting the merry fool and set fair to continue doing so well into the early morning.

Tolerance will also help you to deal good-humouredly with the know-it-all who insists that the wine is 'corked' when you know, beyond all possibility of doubt, that:

(a)   There is nothing wrong with the wine. (His uninformed choice of near-*ordinaire* has not been in the bottle long enough to have become infected, however bad the cork.)

(b)   He has no idea what corked wine tastes like but neard Oz Clark use the expression on TV last week.

(c)   That if you blindfolded him and fed him a glass of milk he would probably pretend to know which side of the hill the grapes had been grown on.

Iron self-control, on the other hand, is needed to deal with the professional complainer, who comes in two guises.

The first is the fellow who gets his kicks from making life a misery for the staff, the proprietor and his fellow diners. He is on a power trip and probably has, concealed about his person, a list of obscure things to complain of in case his memory plays him false. He often comes armed with a copy of the latest food guide, displaying it ostentatiously upon the table and scribbling furiously in a notebook after each exchange with the waiter.

The inexperienced restaurateur is tempted to use placatory techniques on the complainer — anticipating his every whim, taking extra care with each dish served to him and generally ensuring that nothing goes wrong. This is not the way. Your time is better spent attending to your other customers; nice Mr Johnson may not mind waiting a few more minutes but it is never worth the risk of putting a strain on his good nature. The complainer derives no pleasure from the food and wine, only from complaining. He has come to revel in an orgy of whingeing; to demonstrate to anyone foolish enough to take notice that he knows what is what and cannot be fobbed off with excuses and inferior products. He will go right on complaining no matter what you do and by far the best way of dealing with him is to keep him waiting. A good long period of inactivity between courses will, paradoxically, give him something to get his teeth into. And as long as the other customers are all being served promptly he will get no sympathy from them. When he eventually calls for his bill, produce it with alacrity and you will be rid of him.

The second type is more vicious: his objective is a free night out and to this end he will eat his way through a month's salary of food and wine and then engineer a pretext to make a scene and depart without paying the bill. He is adept at exploiting the slenderest of opportunities, and may feign indignation if a person at an adjacent table lights up a cigarette/cigar/pipe; the dining-room can be too hot for him, or too cold, or too noisy. Perhaps he will succeed in provoking the waiter into a caustic retort or insist that the dish he was served was misrepresented on the menu. A practised operator can blow up the most trivial of matters into a major complaint. Legally he is on shaky ground but what are you going to do? Physically restrain him? Call the police? Either of these courses could ruin the evening for your other clients. Damage limitation is the only real option open to you. Tear up his bill and get him out as quickly and quietly as possible, before he puts ideas into someone else's head. If your really must have your revenge, hold him in acrimonious conversation, somewhere out of earshot of the other customers, while the kitchen porter lets his tyres down; but for heaven's sake make sure he gets the right car.

Some of these unwelcome visitors specialize in 'finding' foreign bodies in their food. Fortunately they are rare but we did experience the genre on one occasion, when a woman with a wild and flowing auburn mane 'found' a long, coarse red hair in her salad. The waiters all had short black crops, the only person in the kitchen that day constantly lamented the baby-fine texture of her grey bob so it scarcely required a Sherlock Holmes to deduce the origin of the offending strand, but this did not prevent the woman and her escort from stomping histrionically out of the dining-room, loudly declaiming that they had no intention of paying for contaminated food.

Comparing notes with colleagues over the years we have heard of similar incidents involving flies, beetles and even mouse-droppings.

The magic attribute, and perhaps the one most needed by the professional caterer, is a well-developed sense of humour: desirable at all times and indispensable if you wish to hold on to your staff, your customers and your sanity. The day you can't see the funny side of things is the day you should reassess your suitability for the job.

A wry glance and eyebrows raised in mock exasperation when an inept waiter drops a whole stack of plates in the middle of the dining-room, will have a far more placatory effect on your customers than getting angry with the clumsy idiot. At the first sign of retribution going his way, all sympathy will align itself on his side and you will find yourself in the role of villain.

A sense of humour will also help you to keep your temper when your suppliers spin you colourful and imaginative yarns to account for having let you down yet again, when they have promised faithfully that the goods would be with you tomorrow. But perhaps the greatest gift of all, for those blessed with it, is the ability to go without sleep. The restaurateur/hotelier/landlord who can manage on four hours a night has an inestimable advantage over us poor, normal mortals who need our 'eight straight'.

The hours in the catering trade are not merely unsocial they are also excruciatingly long. Even paying due and proper regard to the licensing laws there are times when you will still be hard at it at two and three a.m. — and even later — but should you permit yourself the luxury of an extra hour in bed while the cleaning staff get the place habitable again, these worthies will snigger amongst themselves and cynically assume that you are sleeping-off the results of a night of drinking and carousing. They will also probably sit around drinking tea and gossiping about you rather than getting on with their work.

It's unfair but, sadly, true that the only way to keep the respect of your staff and get the best from them is never to let them catch you relaxing. Only the knowledge that you work twice as hard and three times as long as they do will induce them grudgingly to forgive you for the double fault of owning the place they only work in and — even worse — pocketing, for your own self-indulgent purposes, every single penny that goes into the till.

'I reckon he made x thousand pounds only last week,' you will overhear them say, if your ears are sharp and alert, but you will never hear them marvel at the size of the bills you have to face — not insignificant among which is the one for their wages.

* * *

The services of an accountant to mediate between you and HM Inspector of Taxes are strongly recommended unless you are yourself qualified in that area. The taxman, who insists that you handle the deduction of taxes from your employees on his behalf, is surprisingly reticent about your ability when it comes to doing your own tax returns.

It is good policy to engage your accountant before you begin trading and allow him to steer you in the way he wishes you to go. He will fairly certainly recommend the precise type of ledger he wishes you to use (or computer program, if you have the necessary hardware, software and expertise in common) and while the one he specifies will not be the only available one that is suited to your purpose — and may even not be the best one — you should humour him nonetheless. If he is dealing with materials that are familiar to him he will be happier, do the job quicker and, with any luck, charge you marginally less.

In the pre-computer — even pre-calculator — dark ages, when we began in the business, our accountant supplied us with a ledger of idiot-proof simplicity. All that he required of us was to enter all the incomings and outgoings in the appropriate columns and add all the figures vertically and horizontally at the end of each week. The total of these was supposed to add up to the same in either direction and to equal the money left in our possession. It rarely did on either count.

The receipts we threw casually into an old shoe-box and once yearly ledger, wages records and shoe-box were driven ceremonially to the accountant's office, where they were checked and correlated and our arithmetic corrected by that season's crop of school-leavers, whose parents were paying good money to have them trained in the science of accountancy.

With the advent of VAT the shoe-box gave way to serious, hard-backed files; receipts were rubber-stamped, dated, numbered, punched and slotted into place in strict numerical sequence. Complex forms had to be completed with meticulous care at three-monthly intervals, giving not only the figures relevant to the calculation of VAT, both paid and collected, but also a whole range of information which we had hitherto regarded as strictly our own business. The purpose of this data-gathering was to allow HM Customs and Excise to compile a vast body of statistics to be used in the furtherance of their mysterious ends or preserved for an uncaring posterity. It took a lot of the fun out of being self-employed.

We could, of course, have paid the accountant to do our returns for us — some of his elderly farmer clients did — but, by that time, the few school-leavers who still regarded accountancy as an acceptable career expected the firms who took them on to pay handsomely for the privilege of imparting their professional knowledge; this expense naturally reflected in the fees, and our bill for their end-of-year services was already quite high enough. We bit the bullet and learned how to cope, and bitterly resented this further intrusion on our valuable time.

There is no substitute for scrupulously-kept records, and keeping them yourself gives you the best possible insight into areas where improvements can be made, and also enables you to see what effect policies such as advertising and staffing levels are having on your takings.

Stock records also need to be kept meticulously if those twin consumers of profits — waste and pilferage — are to be kept to a minimum. Drinks — particularly spirits — and cigarettes head the list of easy pickings and only secure storage facilities and regular monitoring of sales will prevent escalating erosion. Modern morality no longer seriously regards helping oneself to goods left unsupervised as theft and the point has to be clearly made that 'shrinkage' will not go unnoticed.

Perishable stocks should be used in strict rotation and the only way of ensuring this is to organize your storage systems in such a way that the right thing to use is the easiest one to get at. Innate laziness must be made to serve if it is not to undermine.

The health inspector who came with carefully calculated irregularity to investigate our hygiene quotient, looked so squeaky-clean in the white coat he donned before entering that we privately dubbed him the Sanitary Inspector — harking back to our youth and old jokes about smells on the landing. He used a high-tech thermometer to verify the temperature of our fridges and freezers but relied on a more fundamental instrument — his nose — to seek out tell-tale signs of pollution, sticking his head into each and every corner and sampling the air therein with ostentatious sniffs. We kept raw meat and fish in a fridge reserved for this purpose, never allowing them near the cooked food, and everything in the freezers was labelled with the date it was bought. These measures were instituted at the dictate of common sense and the inspector, disappointed by the lost opportunity to lecture us, grudgingly approved them, but he clearly suspected that only the threat of his spot checks kept us from lapsing into unhygienic practices.

These days the preparation and service of food is surrounded by a complex structure of legally enforceable regulations, bolstered by an even vaster web of codes of practice which, though deemed desirable by those in authority who consider themselves qualified to pass such judgements, do not have the force of law. Some of the officials paid to snoop on hard-working unfortunates in the catering business are either unable or unwilling to distinguish between the two categories, with the result that many small businesses are at risk of being crippled by the cost of altering their premises to comply with directives which are not, and perhaps never will be, legally enforceable. It is well worth seeking the advice of a solicitor or the help of trade organizations before meekly agreeing to replace your kitchen tiles with expensive stainless steel cladding.

Your wine reserves should be checked daily if you wish to maintain the credibility of your wine list. It gives a very bad impression when the customer who has chosen, with great care and deliberation, the precise wine that he feels will impress his boss/client/girlfriend, has to be told that the stocks of that particular vintage are exhausted.

Linen stocks, too, have an almost human ability to choose the worst possible moment to run out and, while this should not happen if your staff are properly vigilant, a little extra attention on your part won't come amiss, especially at busy times, when your staff are overstretched.

* * *

If you started out with everything brand, spanking new then it should be a while before you need to set aside a portion of your budget for repairs and renewals, but these should not be forgotten. Electrical equipment, especially, is prone to breakdowns that do not always depend on age or heavy use. Things like your food mixers need servicing regularly and the company that sold them to you will probably arrange a contract. Incidentally, don't be fooled by the grand phrase 'subject to commercial warranty'; this does not, as you might possibly expect, signify a longer period of guarantee than domestic machines. Quite the contrary — it usually means your equipment is covered against failure for six months only, rather than the year that domestic appliances enjoy. Considering the immense cost of robust commercial equipment this seems most unfair.

A regular count of your glassware, crockery and silver is a wise precaution to avoid panic ordering of replacements. Even with average care breakages do mount up and, at busy times, cutlery has been known to disappear into the waste-bins along with the food scraps. A monthly census will sharpen the awareness of those who have the handling of these things.

And do make sure that there is a special bin for broken glass and crockery. Should such items find their way into the plastic rubbish bags and inflict a cut on the hand of a refuse collector (what happened to dustmen?) you could face a claim for lost potential earnings of jackpot proportions if he manages to secure the right legal advice.

And, finally, keep a sharp eye on the decorative state of your premises; seeing it every day it is easy to become accustomed to small blemishes in the paint and wear to the carpet in heavy traffic areas. Try to see it with the eyes of a new customer every time you enter the front door, the bar or the dining-room, and do make a point of actually using the customer lavatories occasionally — just sticking your head round the door to make sure the cleaner has done her job is not enough, you need to examine them from the same angle as the users. Soap stalactites under the wash-basin are often only noticeable from a sitting position.

CHAPTER TWELVE

THE LICENSING LAWS

Before presuming to give advice on the subject of the licensing laws we approached our solicitor for a few hard facts. When he had finally managed to control his mirth he took down several kilos of relevant material, bound in four massive volumes and couched in the usual impenetrable morass of legal language, and offered us the use of a corner of his office in which to study them. We were, we told him, thinking more along the lines of a résumé set out in colloquial form. He rolled his eyes skyward in a gesture intended to convey that even his understanding of this mine-strewn subject was not without limits and frankly he didn't fancy our chances of reducing it to agony aunt proportions.

If you buy premises which already have a licence in operation then the solicitor who does your conveyancing will deal with the relevant forms that are required to effect the transfer of that licence. The local police will supply you with literature setting out the commandments contained in the laws relating to the sale of alcohol and specifying the circumstances in which you can expect to get a severe knuckle-rapping — or worse. If you are applying for a new licence it is even more advisable to involve a solicitor and let him do the worrying.

With regard to such matters as obtaining extensions — permits to extend the hours of service for special occasions — if you have joined a trade organization they will be able to deal with these things for you, and when the time comes for the licence to be renewed you will be notified well in advance by the courts as to the date on which the said renewal will be dealt with. Any attempt to set out a clear picture of what is involved in this rag-bag of legislation would be labour lost, since changes are constantly being made, so the best advice we can give is to read as much up-to-date material as you can lay your hands on when the time comes.

The licensing laws of this country exist for the purpose of regulating every aspect of the sale of alcohol and basically they dictate when, in what quantities and to whom it may be sold. The when — known as permitted hours — dates back no further than the First World War, when the restrictions were introduced with the aim of discouraging the munition workers, and others whose efforts were essential to the war effort, from lingering in the pubs, squandering their unaccustomedly high wages on drink, instead of getting back to work.

The restrictions regarding the amounts and measures by which it may be dispensed are intended, presumably, to keep landlords honest and prevent them from profiting unfairly from the customer's loss of perception, which is progressively worsened by each drink he imbibes. The antiquity in which these measures are rooted is reflected in their names — gills, firkins, hogsheads, et cetera.

Beer must be sold in exact measures of a pint, half-pint or one-third-pint — or, in the case of a yard of ale, a quart. The glasses in which it is served must, by law, contain exactly the correct amount, which means that they must be filled to the brim — a fact which gives rise to acrimonious discussion about whether or not the head is an integral part of the pint and what margin of froth is permissible. Strictly speaking the law does not allow any; should you however, in an attempt to abide strictly by the letter of it, fill the glass to such an extent that the froth rises above the rim and begins to run down the sides, you are then in danger of giving marginally more than the exact amount and thus committing the heinous offence know as 'the long pull'. In the eyes of the licensing authorities, generosity is just as reprehensible as stinginess and carries a penalty, on conviction, of £100 (according to the most up-to-date reference booklet we could find).

Gin, whisky, rum and vodka may only be sold in measures of one-fourth, one-fifth or one-sixth of a gill or — in nodding acknowledgement of our European commitment — twenty-five millilitres. Brandy, however, is not included in the list and may presumably be served in any quantity you wish, including sloshing it, with careless abandon, into cut crystal goldfish bowls if your customers are prepared to pay the price.

There are no rules about quantity when wine is served by the glass — anything from a liqueur thimble to a pint pot will pass, if you can get away with it — nor are you under any obligation to make your customers privy to the size of vessel you intend to use, nor the extent to which you intend to fill it, unless they specifically ask you. Should you serve the same wine in a carafe, however, and permit the customer to pour it into his own glass, that carafe must, by law, contain a quarter of a litre, a half-pint, or multiples thereof.

* * *

Those to whom alcohol may be served are more simply and easily defined. It is an offence to serve alcohol to a person under the age of eighteen years or to permit another to buy alcohol for such a person to consume on the premises. A certain discretion is allowed in prosecuting such an offence if the licensee can show that he had no reason to suspect that the person involved was, in fact, under age. The statuesque blonde, with the forty-inch bust and dripping diamonds and sables, who enters your bar on the arm of an elder statesman could, just possibly, be a day or two short of her eighteenth birthday, but would you dare to ask?

The other proscribed category is anyone who has already had far too much. The problem with this one is that it is a matter of opinion — in your opinion he is roaring drunk and certainly shouldn't have any more; in his opinion he hasn't even started yet. The outcome probably depends on which view carries the most conviction behind it or — should the police become involved — before it.

There is no legal obligation to close licensed premises at any time, provided that alcohol is only sold during the hours permitted. This information is academic — by closing time you will be only too glad to get them all out, shut up shop and, if you are lucky, put your feet up, or get on with a thousand and one other jobs if you are not. Alcohol purchased in a bar during permitted hours may continue to be consumed for a period not exceeding twenty minutes following the calling of 'time'. In the case of someone who is eating a meal a further ten minutes is graciously added to the twenty, giving him half an hour to finish savouring the last of his bottle of wine or drink up the hastily-ordered brandies.

Residents may buy and consume alcohol at any hour of the day or night; bear that in mind, and temper your language, when the chap in number forty-three comes knocking on your bedroom door at four a.m. to insist on exercising his legal right to buy another bottle of whisky.

You, the licensee, also have the right to drink, and entertain your (bona fide) friends, outside permitted hours — though the rules stipulate that this must be strictly at your own expense. You may even ply your employees with strong liquor if you be so minded — again at your own expense only. We trust it will be a comfort to you, when you find your staff have been pilfering, that you can't be prosecuted for allowing them to drink out of hours, since they did so at your expense.

The language in which much of the licensing law is couched is quaint and colourful. There is the serious offence, for example, of harbouring and, more specifically, harbouring a constable.

Harbouring consists of knowingly permitting a common prostitute or a known thief or a constable who is not there in the execution of his duty, to remain upon licensed premises.

The reasons for excluding the first two categories is fairly self-evident, but it is left to the imagination to conjure up a picture of the unbridled excesses which might result from allowing a constable unfettered access to premises where strong drink is sold.

Chief constables are not included in this restriction — neither are sergeants nor detective inspectors nor other exalted ranks — they are allowed to waste time and public money drinking in bars throughout the full gamut of permitted hours without any interference from the august body that frames the laws they are committed to upholding.

A constable who is off duty and wearing civilian clothes ceases to be a constable in the eyes of the licensing laws. A slightly contradictory element is introduced by the fact that the licensee is legally required to permit a constable on duty to enter the premises during licensing hours, including the drinking-up period, in order to detect or prevent crime — scope for interpretation there — and at other times if they have reason to believe that an offence is being committed therein. The quoted penalty for this one is £50 but, as we have no figure for the tariff levied on harbouring, we are unable to advise on the best course to follow if there is conflicting evidence as to his real motives.

Permitted hours, nowadays, run from 11 a.m. to 11 p.m. except on Sundays, Christmas Day and Good Friday, when they begin at noon until 3 p.m. and resume at 7 p.m. to finish at 10.30. Under certain circumstances and subject to a series of complicated conditions the normal hours may be extended. Even on the holy days some latitude is theoretically possible, though the regulations pertaining thereto are so hedged about with 'subject only to' and 'according to the requirements of' that we couldn't be sure of where, when and how. From the little we were able to comprehend, if you live in Wales or Monmouthshire it's probably not worth the trouble of applying.

* * *

Being an innkeeper carries serious obligations. An innkeeper is defined as the keeper of an establishment that purports to offer food, drink and, where appropriate, sleeping accommodation to any bona fide traveller who apparently has the means to pay for same and is in a fit state to be so accommodated. This obligation does not extend to every restaurant which has a couple of rooms for overnight guests but those of you who have succumbed to Ye Olde Coaching Inne, or any of its updates, should look to the terms of your licence.

The Hotel Proprietors Act of 1956 stipulates (we paraphrase) that the innkeeper must receive all and sundry, at any hour of the day or night, until such time as his inn is bursting at the seams. Personalities are not allowed to enter into it — any bona fide traveller who is neither inebriated nor verminous (and I imagine that nowadays one may include: under the influence of illegal drugs) must be accommodated, whether or not you like the cut of his jib. Opening an upstairs window at three a.m., in response to a loud knocking on your door, and yelling, 'Get lost, you lousy drunk!' is not regarded as a proper and legal way of indicating that, in your considered opinion, he is in no fit state to be received.

Precisely how the modern innkeeper is supposed to know

whether or not someone is a bona fide traveller, in this tag-end of the twentieth century, is not explained. In earlier times, when horse-power moved on four legs, or multiples thereof, travellers were easily identified; they were the ones who hopped off a passing stage-coach, or rode up, covered in dust, on a mud-spattered, sweat-stained nag, crying loudly: 'Ostler, kindly stable my horse!' Nowadays, when it is not considered in the least eccentric to get into one's car and travel fifty yards to the end of the street to buy a newspaper, the genuine traveller is less clearly defined.

The carrying of suitcases gives a clue of sorts and is also helpful in that the innkeeper is empowered to hang on to the guest's belongings, should he fail to pay his bill. Once he has taken the precaution of advertising his intentions in one London and one local paper, the innkeeper may sell the goods following a period of six weeks.

Don't, however, be lulled into a sense of false security by the Mercedes, with a king's ransom worth of golf-clubs on the back seat, parked in your yard; vehicles and their contents are off-limits in the sequestration stakes.

There are various stipulations regarding the licensee's liabilities, and the proper way of limiting these is by the use of disclaimer notices but once you have cut through the 'whereby's and the 'here-to-fore's, many of the calamities that can befall can be prevented by such common-sense measures as proper lighting on stairways and the prompt replacement of fraying carpets.

* * *

The section headed 'Intoxicating Liquors' defines the minimum level of alcoholic content required for a drink to qualify for restriction on the hours during which it may be offered for sale, and lists those substances which are exempt. Perfume, vanilla essence and 'spirits, wine or made-wine so medicated as to be, in the opinion of the Commissioners, intended for use as a medicine' may be sold and drunk without regard to the time of day. In the case of the latter, however, since the opinion of the Commissioners is rarely printed on the label, it might be safer to consult them and get confirmation in writing before passing the Wincarnis.

A further unrestricted substance is any liquor of a gravity not exceeding 1,016 degrees and containing no more than 1.2% alcohol. Note, however, that this category does not cover whisky drowned in a sufficiently diluting quantity of soda. Watering the drinks comes under the heading of adulteration and incurs heavy penalties.

'Thou shalt not commit adulteration' is number three in the licensees' decalogue.

The giving of credit by a licensee in respect of drinks is illegal. Where the drinks are supplied for consumption with a meal, or ancillary to it, they may be paid for at the termination of said meal and if the recipient is resident on the premises then they may be added to his bill; otherwise it's money up front every time. It is also illegal to accept goods as security for spirits sold; if Joe Bloggs has run out of funds but is desperate for one more double, you could be putting your licence at risk by accepting his watch as a pledge, so don't even consider it — even if it is a Rolex. Come to think of it, especially if it is a Rolex; under the circumstances it's probably a fake.

The licensing laws are universally unpopular, except with the brewers, who have always been reluctant to see them rescinded. During the period when we were transforming our first premises from run-down country pub to attractive restaurant we kept the public bar open to maintain the licence and we regularly found that almost 50 per cent of our takings crossed the bar during the last ten minutes before time was called. We were convinced that much of that money would not have been spent had the customers not been aware of the impending deadline.

The licensing laws are also a field in which experts abound among the general public. All manner of fanciful interpretations of them will be put to you in support of pleas for out-of-hours drinks and other concessions. There are times when it is tempting to yield to these blandishments, especially when they come from exceptionally high-spending customers. The best way to protect yourself is to acquire an unassailable knowledge of the facts, insofar as this is possible, including the stance taken by your local enforcement body, and then practise blind and unwavering obedience to the eleventh commandment: 'Thou shalt not get found out.'

CHAPTER THIRTEEN

RESIDENTS

So far we have said little about the residential side—the letting of rooms to guests who stay overnight or longer.

People staying on the premises complicate the business but do not materially alter it. It is important, however, to balance the potential extra profit against the work and expense involved.

The cost of appointing the rooms will be quite high — people nowadays expect a good standard of comfort, including *en suite* bathrooms. (With such a rich language of our own, was it really necessary to concoct an adjective out of a couple of nondescript syllables borrowed from French, in order to convey this particular form of contiguousness; as if the French — of all people — invented the concept?)

There will be rooms to be cleaned, linen to be changed, and breakfasts to prepare. And bear in mind that a responsible person must be on the premises at all times when guests are in residence; your already long working day will be stretched even further by guests who are legally entitled to drink all night if they wish, and may, indeed, do so, since they don't have to drive home.

Breakfast *à l'Anglaise* does not, of course, require a fully-trained chef to prepare it, but the fact remains that somebody has to get up and do it and, unless you have a place separate from the dining-room in which it can be served, there will be days when the guests linger over coffee and the morning papers and hold up the process of cleaning and preparing for lunch.

And to all this must be added the cost of complying with the fire regulations — yet another morass of legislation along similar lines to the licensing laws. They differ from the latter however, in that they are 'open to interpretation'. Alan has had the most recent experience in this field, having been involved in refurbishing and re-opening a country hotel restaurant — a charming converted manor, with spacious, elegant rooms, standing in extensive grounds, which had been allowed, over a period of years, to become rundown. The account of his experiences, written in vitriol while the scars were still unhealed, has been heavily bowdlerized before inclusion in this chapter.

The ink has barely dried on the protection order — a promising name for what is nothing more than a temporary licence, granted to a new licensee to tide him over until the next full licensing sessions — when the fire officer is on the phone requesting an appointment to look over the premises and assess the fire-risks inherent therein.

At the duly appointed hour he presents himself at the entrance and offers a distracted hand to be shaken — his professional eye is already sizing up the doorway. Behind him stands a junior fireman, adolescently spotty, his body somewhat at odds with the nearest regulation size of uniform. His name is Joseph and his role is clearly defined: he is there to carry the battered portfolio containing leaflets and a dog-eared, out-of-date copy of the fire regulations, to hold the other end of the tape measure and to agree vociferously with every opinion uttered by his superior.

The officer drags his gaze from the front door, nodding smiling approval; the door complies with the specifications required of a main exit and he is delighted to start the proceedings off on an up-beat note. The mood, however, is short-lived; he runs his tape across the glass inner-door that protects the foyer from the icy blast which accompanies each new arrival, then checks it a second time, as if unwilling to accept his own findings.

'Three inches too narrow to comply with the requirements of . . .' (he reels off a series of letters and figures and flaps a hand at Joseph to pass the relevant leaflet from the portfolio).

'That's right,' says Joseph hopefully, riffling through the papers.

There is a second exit from the foyer leading to the garden; perhaps this will compensate for the inches lacking in the main one?

'Not unless it is wide enough to comply with the regulations; they make no provision for multiple exits — merely stipulate the minimum width main exits must be.'

'That's right,' says Joseph — still unable to substantiate this opinion with the elusive reference.

The auxiliary lights — there to show up the exits in the event of the power failing during an emergency — are tested and respond promptly. They, at least, are satisfactory? Again the doubtful head-shake. 'According to British Standard number . . .' (Joseph steps up his search) 'I doubt if they'll conform strictly to the specifications when they're tested by a qualified electrician.'

They lit up when required; what more could one ask of a light bulb?

'These British Standards have to be met' (the tone implies 'or the Empire might crumble') 'according to section . . . er . . . of the Act — have you got it there Joseph?' Joseph opines that it is among that lot we left back at the station.

'Oh well, never mind. You can buy copies of all the booklets from the bookstore in the new shopping centre; they stock all the Ministry publications.' He fails to mention that these sell for the sort of sums that used only to be quoted in guineas.

The alarm system is basic, but probably just about complies with the BS basic standard stipulated by the rules.

'But it'll need rewiring and while you're having that done you might as well up-grade to BS . . . er . . .' (Joseph continues to go through the motions) 'for a small extra cost you will then be prepared for when the standard basic requirement is up-graded.'

'Absolutely,' says Joseph, diversifying.

The kitchen is equipped with extinguishers, fire-blankets and buckets of sand.

'You'll need to have those extinguishers serviced regularly and produce a certificate. I think we might just get away with that particular model — it's marginal but it might just pass . . .'

Joseph smiles and nods. The fire officer is a good chap really — doing his best for you; bending the regulations ever so slightly in your favour.

'It's all a matter of interpretation, really.'

Joseph keeps his own council — interpretation is outside his sphere of influence.

The fire-blankets are obsolete — superseded by the new, miracle fabric referred to in para . . .

'No, I'm wrong. It's not in yet — too new — so these are still acceptable, but when you renew them . . .'

The grade of sand in the buckets goes unchallenged.

At the foot of the elegant, hand-carved oak staircase the fire officer pauses, lost in admiration.

'That's a fine staircase; we certainly don't want to spoil that, do we?'

Joseph — not strong on architectural appreciation — gives a barely perceptible shrug.

'Tell you what we can do. We can put double fire-doors here in this archway. That will protect the upper floor, in compliance with the Act, without damaging the stairs.'

With fire-doors in that archway, the staircase — the most delightful feature of the entire building — will be seen only by customers on their way to the lavatories and, by the time they have fought their way through the weighty, heavily-sprung obstruction, even they will probably have eyes for nothing but their destination.

Throughout all this the fire officer is noting down figures intended to guide him when the moment comes to advise on the cost of all these acts of compliance.

Up the stairs he makes a tour of the bedrooms available for letting; the manager's flat holds no interest for him — in common with private cinema clubs screening pornographic films it doesn't come within the scope of the Act. Private premises, those are. No, you and your six children are not included in the number of persons resident for the purposes of fire-risk assessment. That's a relief! Had he inspected the kitchen he would have been appalled by the sight of toaster, kettle and microwave, all piggy-backed into double adapters, sharing the solitary 13-amp socket.

Extra illuminated 'Exit' signs will be insisted upon, he thinks. 'Regulation number . . . er . . . states that . . . Joseph?' (the frantic riffling continues).

'He's only been in the job a week,' the senior man confides in a stage whisper.

The hotel has, at some stage, been extended by the addition of a small wooden building which serves as an office, and from a first-floor balcony a wide wrought-iron fire-escape of Victorian design runs across the timber roof of this extension and down to the garden.

'A fire-escape? No, I don't think you'll need one. The regulations don't . . . Oh, there is one? Let's go and take a look.'

Brownie points at last! This is a bonus that he can put in his report — a supernumerary fire-escape! Surely that will compensate for those three missing inches? Back down in the garden the duo surveys the handsome structure, crafted during the golden age of decorative iron-work. Breath is sucked in through tightly clenched teeth. It's a splendid feature: robust, sound as a bell — far superior to these modern designs — but that wooden extension underneath it . . . (the heads shake in unison) that would go up like a bomb if it caught fire. The fire-escape above it would be turned into a grid-iron upon which guests, fleeing to safety, would be barbecued. Either fire-escape or wooden building will have to go. And no, blocking-off the entrance won't help.

'As long as it's there, people will assume it's to be used. Precious time could be lost . . .'

Joseph nods vigorously; he may be new to the service but even he is aware of the danger of losing time in a conflagration situation.

'And if you decide to keep it, it will have to be roofed over. Otherwise, in winter it will become a hazard. People escaping from a fire could slip on snow or ice and sustain injury.'

What an agonizing choice — twisted ankles versus roasting to death.

What will all this add up to?

'Well, you understand, I can only give you a rough idea —

105

my report will go to my chief and he will interpret it and make his recommendations according to Section . . .' (he has given up expecting documentary support from Joseph) 'but I should think you may get away with spending twenty . . . twenty-five perhaps. No, that's thousands, not hundreds.' He and Joseph exchange smirks.

'Yes, I know it's a rather large investment but at least you will have the peace of mind of knowing that you have done everything possible to protect your guests. And, of course, it will be reflected in your insurance premiums.'

Twenty-five thousand divided by how many years?

'But anyway, the chief will make his recommendations in the light of the provisions in the Act — he has all the up-to-date information to hand. Well, no, he's not likely to take the extra exits into account — he works strictly to the book.

'However, these regulations do not apply to buildings where less than seven guests — or staff members — are accommodated.

'The staff live in a cottage in the grounds, you say?

'Well, in that case — I'm speaking unofficially now, you understand — in your shoes I would convert one of the four bedrooms to storage and just let the other three. Save you a lot of hassle.'

We don't know to what extent our brushes with petty officialdom are typical. It may just be our unpronounceable, foreign-sounding name that throws them off balance, or perhaps they are baffled by our sense of humour. We do, however, know that, through the years, we have heard them described in colourful and even forceful language by frustrated colleagues engaged in the vain pursuit of the permits, certificates, licences or simply the information that they need, so that they may go lawfully about their business.

There are social rewards, as well as monetary, in playing host to residential guests. We have spent many pleasant evenings, drinking wine and conversing with the more *sympatique* of the boarders, after the day-pupils had gone home.

Whether to let rooms or not is a matter for personal preference set against financial need. Once you have sat down and worked out to what extent the rewards can be expected to outweigh the expenditure in investment and trouble, you will be able to decide if it is worthwhile. But remember that there will always be a 'hidden agenda' and the initial calculations can never take account of every item which must be budgeted for.

There is, by the way, a legal obligation to keep a register of guests for the benefit of the police, even though they no longer have the manpower to come around and check it on a regular basis as they used to. In addition to this register many places keep a visitors' book for guests to sign, giving them the opportunity to browse through it and see if there are any famous names included.

CHAPTER FOURTEEN

EULOGY

After all the warnings and forebodings that have gone before, we propose to end on a positive note and try to explain why, in spite of everything, we stayed in the business for thirty years and, given the chance to go back in time, would probably be fool enough to do it all over again. Notwithstanding the things that can — and invariably do — go wrong, there is nothing to match the pleasure and satisfaction when things go gloriously, spectacularly right.

Like that birthday dinner, when the food is inspired and the host has chosen (with your guidance) the perfect wines to complement it; when the chef has surpassed himself and produced a birthday gateau that merits exhibition in the Tate Gallery and all the little touches you have so thoughtfully added — place-cards, posies for the ladies and hand-made chocolates with the coffee — have not gone unnoticed. And the tip that the birthday-girl's husband adds cheerfully when settling the bill has the staff wondering if it is their birthday too.

The promises to come back and do it again the next time someone has a birthday come floating back on the night air, as the guests drift contentedly back to their cars, and leave a warm glow that carries you through the clearing up, if not on a rosy cloud, at least with the feeling that it is a worthwhile profession after all.

There are the evenings when your guests depart, thanking you for a marvellous evening, just as if they were private dinner-guests and had not just paid a hefty bill for the meal they are praising so highly. Some of them will say, 'You must come and dine with us one evening — on your closing-day perhaps.'

Some of them will even mean it — though they tend to spoil the effect by adding, 'Of course, we couldn't offer you food like we eat here.' Don't they realize that you'd be out of business if they could?

* * *

When we took time off to go to France to shop for luxuries, in the pre-EC days when some ingredients were still difficult to get over here, there was never any shortage of volunteers to accompany us.

'You'll show us all the best places to eat,' they would gush, Michelin stars in their eyes. It required considerable tact to persuade them, without making them feel unwelcome, that *Laperouse* and the *Tour d'Argent* were not on the agenda and that our idea of a holiday meal was a fluffy omelette with a crisp salad bathed in the sort of *vinaigrette* dressing that the French are born knowing how to make, a tray piled high with local cheeses and an abundant supply of the regional wine, at a modest village *auberge*.

Which was not to say that, should our route take us within pilgrimage distance of the town of Vienne on the way south, we would not treat ourselves to one glorious meal at *Le Pyramide*, but otherwise it was strictly the *Menu a cinquante francs*.

* * *

We met some delightful people: the adorable couple in their seventies who had never been abroad in their lives, who came for a few wide-eyed, wonder-struck days in Paris and were so reluctant to come home that we extended our stay and took them to visit the *chateaux* of the Loire. Taking a pair of charming, well-behaved children on their first trip to Disneyland couldn't possibly be as rewarding.

There were many memorable customers who stood out from the crowd. One local businessman, son of a French mother, and fluent in the language, cast our restaurant in the role of his personal staff canteen and came almost daily to lunch. He even managed to sweet-talk the chef into serving him chips with his *tournedos* — the nearest anyone else got was *pommes allumettes* with their grouse. He resented, on our behalf, any customer who was being difficult or tiresome and would make disparaging remarks about them in French. On one occasion, when his target announced loudly that he had a perfect understanding of that language, our champion promptly switched to equally fluent Spanish. The tiresome one departed, vowing that the food guides would hear of the incident. We have no idea if they ever did but, since we were constantly in their bad books anyway, we didn't lose any sleep over it.

Another couple of regular visitors were childless in middle-age and had developed a taste for the good things of the table that far outstripped their income. Fortunately their four sets of grandparents had all been blessed with a fecundity not inherited by their progeny and, as time took its toll of a succession of barren aunts and uncles, the resulting legacies were joyously squandered in our dining-room.

Then there was the retired doctor, avidly Francophile, who had reached an age where fragile health kept him and his wife from making the gastronomic journeys they had enjoyed since the end of the war opened up the Channel routes once again. They designated us an outpost of France and came monthly to dine, stay overnight and lunch on the following day before making the sixty-mile journey home. While they ate their light luncheon before leaving, they would study the menu and decide on the delights they were going to look forward to eating on their next visit.

We were not overwhelmed with tourists, but two American couples stick out in our memories. The first, a charming, cultured man with an equally delightful wife, chatted with us far into the night on a variety of subjects ranging from history, through gastronomy, to the influence of Greek and Latin on modern languages, raising a number of questions we were obliged to leave unanswered.

Some months later we received a letter, written on the stationery of the Library of Congress, in Washington, thanking us for a pleasant and stimulating stay and enclosing some photocopied extracts from rare and ancient books, which threw light on some of the outstanding queries. He had obviously gone to a great deal of trouble and for a long period we corresponded sporadically in between their five-yearly visits.

The other couple, young, shy and unsure of themselves but anxious to try something new, came in the late spring and ordered fresh asparagus. They had taken the precaution of checking with Emily Post's manual of etiquette for the correct way to eat this unfamiliar vegetable but, unfortunately, had slightly misinterpreted her advice. They confidently cut off the tender green tips and laid them to one side of the plate and then, taking each spear delicately between finger and thumb, chewed their way laboriously through the woody stalks. We did not have the heart to ask if they enjoyed them but couldn't resist taking the plates, with the rejected tips, back to the kitchen to see the chef's mystified reaction.

* * *

Perhaps the most outstanding meal we ever prepared — and the occasion which is still evoked whenever two or more members of our now-defunct dining-club are gathered together — was in honour of the sixtieth birthday of our wine-merchant. Born on the anniversary of the Battle of Waterloo, wine is his business, his hobby and his continuing source of pleasure. His Pickwickian, bow-fronted shop is rarely without a small gathering of like-minded friends who have come to buy and stayed to taste and, whenever we pay him a visit, his greeting is drowned by the sound of a cork being drawn.

The meal in question was chosen with great care and deliberation, to match the breathtaking collection of wines he had got together for the occasion — a cart-before-the-horse situation and a challenge we thoroughly enjoyed.

The evening began with *Dom Pérignon* 1976 and the meal itself started with a dish of scallops and pike *quenelles*, married with *Chateau Grillet* '81 — a connoiseurs' white wine from the *Côte Rôtie* area. The tiny, four-acre estate which produces it is the smallest vineyard in France to have its own *Appellation Controlée*.

After this we served whole truffles in a fine pastry crust, atop slices of *foie gras*, with a 1966 *Le Montrachet*; then came

111

a *Morey-St.-Denis* — also '66 — with a whole sirloin and wing-rib of beef, charred outside and showing rare and succulent as it was carved at the table. The cheeses — selected for their mildness so as not to overshadow it — accompanied the venerable, and still surprisingly powerful, *Chateau Leoville Poyferre* 1880, which had Alan trembling at the knees as he drew the crumbling corks.

The dessert wine, served with individual *crèmes brulées*, made extra special by a coronet of spun sugar, was the same age as the guest of honour — a 1924 *Chateau Rieussec*, but the most remarkable wine of the evening was the *Madeira Bual* that circulated at the end of the meal instead of the customary port; its vintage was 1815, the year the Battle of Waterloo was fought. Ten years on, there are still many to whom 'Henry's Sixtieth' remains the yardstick of gastronomic excellence.

We could go on and on reminiscing, but we would be preaching to the converted; dreamers need no prompting from us to imagine all the joys and delights to be derived from running a restaurant. We can only hope that our little exposé of the grimmer realities that are inextricably interwoven with the pleasures will help them to temper their expectations and enjoy their venture into the world of catering to the public as much as we enjoyed ours.